Faces and Figures in American Drawings

By

E. Maurice Bloch

An Exhibition in the
Virginia Steele Scott Gallery
The Huntington Library and Art Gallery
January through April, 1989

Library of Congress No. 88 – 35772
ISBN 0 – 87328 – 127 – 6

The Huntington Library and Art Gallery
San Marino, California

Preface

Drawings by American artists have not received the sustained, comprehensive attention from collectors, scholars, and museums that for many generations has been devoted to European drawings. This situation has changed as the interest in American art of all kinds has grown during the past two decades. But American drawings remain a field as yet relatively unexplored. It is, accordingly, a privilege for the Huntington Library, Art Collections, and Botanical Gardens to present, at its Virginia Steele Scott Gallery for American art, the first in a projected series of three exhibitions of American drawings from the collection of E. Maurice Bloch.

Dr. Bloch has devoted a distinguished academic career to the history of American art and the general field of graphic arts. At the same time, as a private collector, he has assembled, with modest means guided by a connoisseur's eye and a scholar's knowledge, a highly important, representative group of American drawings numbering several hundred sheets. He has generously agreed to share with the public this collection and the wealth of information he has accumulated concerning it.

The present exhibition, selected and catalogued by Dr. Bloch, concentrates on portrait and figure drawings from the late eighteenth century through the early twentieth. In the Introduction he explores the interesting but neglected topic of the history of collecting American drawings.

Robert Wark
Curator of the Huntington Art Collections

By the late eighteenth and early nineteenth century a tradition for collecting drawings had already enjoyed a long and established history in Europe. England, in particular, was an important center for collecting drawings, notably for the succession of distinguished painter-collectors, such as Lely, the Richardsons, Reynolds, and Lawrence, who were all considered connoisseurs of the medium. American-born Benjamin West formed a celebrated collection of Old Master drawings during his long residence in England. In all probability inspired by Reynolds' example, he collected them for personal study, as well as for the students working under his direction at the Royal Academy. More than his predecessors, his own drawing practice echoes the mannerisms and techniques of Guercino, Parmigianino, and Castiglione, who were all well represented in the collection. He seems not, however, to have collected drawings by his contemporaries.

In America, at least in West's lifetime, the collecting of drawings on a comparable scale, was almost non-existent. The remarkable exceptions were James Bowdoin III, whose collection was bequeathed to Bowdoin College in 1811, and Robert Gilmor, Jr. of Baltimore.[1] Since both men traveled extensively abroad, the pattern of their collecting tended to reflect European taste and laid stress on the Old Masters. Bowdoin also had a family collection of portraits by American colonial painters, and Gilmor was among the pioneers in collecting contemporary Americans along with the Europeans; but their drawing collections include none by Americans.[2] The tendency, at least among native artists of the time, was to regard drawing as an exercise, or merely incidental to the execution of a painting. With important exceptions of West and Copley, who became first-rate draftsmen after they left America, native artists of the time displayed little or no interest in drawing as a primary art form. The American students who gained access to West's collection had almost certainly never seen an Old Master drawing before. They were rarely preserved in America, and collectors like Bowdoin and Gilmor acquired their holdings during their travels abroad.

Up to this point there was little to excite interest in American draftsmanship of any kind. The first concentrated attempt to direct attention to the importance of drawing should be credited to Samuel F.B. Morse, who joined forces with Thomas S. Cummings, William Dunlap, and Frederick Agate in the formation of the Society for Improvement in Drawing in New York during the late fall of 1825. Morse and his artist colleagues felt compelled to take the initiative at that time after receiving repeated complaints from students of the American Academy school then administered by the venerable artist-patriot John Trumbull. It appeared evident to them that no serious effort was being made by the old Academy to find competent instructors; nor indeed were any instructors or facilities readily accessible at reasonable times to those students who came to draw from the collection of casts. The students were clearly being left to their own resources. Morse took the lead in recognizing the urgency of the problem.

The first meeting of the Society, probably the first of a drawing society ever held in this country, resulted in the evolution of the New-York Drawing Association. This organization agreed to provide a room and models to aspiring artists who were required to supply their own materials and pay a five-dollar membership fee. Though it was a bold stroke at the time, a serious confrontation with the Academy was easily predictable and soon forthcoming. When Trumbull himself attempted to interfere with the proceedings of the new Association, the artists retaliated by rejecting any further connection with the old Academy and countered by forming the National Academy of Design in January, 1826. As might have been expected, Morse was elected its first President.[3]

Morse's personal understanding of the value of basic drawing came from a long-remembered experience as a favored student of West at the Royal Academy. This he was to carry over in his own teaching, and he must have played a leading role in instituting a formal drawing curriculum in the newly-formed Academy school. It can also be no coincidence that drawing as an art form was soon afterward brought to public attention in the Academy's annual exhibitions. Beginning in 1827, when Henry Jackson Morton exhibited two drawings, the works of American draftsmen can be identified sporadically in shows throughout the 1830s but, by 1845, the appearance of drawings and watercolors had become a regular occurrence.[4]

The emphasis on drawing was further underlined when, a year after the Academy was established, the members themselves organized The Sketch Club. Evidently designed to take up where the New-York Drawing Association left off, it was founded by Morse, Durand, Ingham, and Cummings and came in time to be known as the Twenty-one or The Old Sketch Club, the former title reflecting a limited membership which was increased in later years.[5] With the objective of the association broadened to include an intermingling of patrons of art and men of letters, the Club tended to become a somewhat more elite and social group than its earlier counterpart.[6] The location of alternate Friday evening meetings rotated among the members who acted as hosts in providing simple refreshment and the privilege of selecting the subject of a one-hour drawing which each host could also claim as his own. Due to the character of the membership, however, its sketching activity had all but ceased by 1846.[7] Although The Sketch Club endured for more than twenty years afterward, another organization, The Artists' Sketching Club, which was seriously devoted to drawing, had already taken its place. Organized in January 1844, it met once a week in a room provided by the National Academy. In this instance, a monitor gave out the subject for a one-hour drawing session, and the drawings were afterward collected and exhibited before being returned to their owners. Although this club was short-lived, the identity and sincere purpose of sketching societies persisted, and the idea of collecting drawings seems to have evolved out of them.

The earliest surviving gatherings of drawings were not collections in the modern sense but drawings that were exchanged in one way or another by artist-friends. The "collections" of Thomas Seir Cummings (1804-1894) and John Ludlow Morton (1792-1871), which have survived, are classic examples of the kind. The Cummings Album, which was dispersed some twenty years ago in the art market, included sketches by several of the most prominent artists working in New York in 1827, precisely the time when The Sketch Club was being formed under the auspices of the National Academy. Cummings was one of its founders, as well as a founding-father and treasurer of the Academy, a position he was to hold for forty years. Since Cummings is recorded as host on at least one of the Club's sketch evenings, we may also assume that his "album" of drawings by Inman, Cole, Wall, Henry Jackson Morton, and John Ludlow Morton became his property on that occasion.[8]

The John Ludlow Morton Sketchbook, now in the New-York Historical Society, which dates from about 1827-1830, contains twenty-five drawings of small size, and is apparently intact. Like Cummings, apparently a close friend, Morton was a painter who was among the first fifteen members of the new Academy, its first Corresponding Secretary and, incidentally, also a member of the Academy's first Antique Class. His "sketchbook," which includes twenty-five highly finished drawings by artists who were all personal friends and colleagues—Morse, Durand, Edmonds, Ingham, Agate, Flagg, Cole, Sully, and Weir—may have been assembled for presentation to Morton to commemorate a special occasion rather than the end product of a casual evening of sketch club activity.[9]

Probably the earliest true collection of drawings by American artists can be credited to Charles Lanman (1819-1895), an aspiring writer and artist who arrived in New York from Norwich, Connecticut in 1835. During the ten years he remained in the city, he supported himself as a clerk for a mercantile house while entertaining thoughts about becoming a serious artist. He studied painting under Asher B. Durand, exhibited one of his landscapes for the first time at the National Academy in 1840 and, within two years, was elected an Associate Member. During this period, he also began a career as an art critic. His perceptive article on "Cole's Imaginative Paintings" appeared in 1843,[10] and a more expansive one "Our New-York Painters" was published the following year,[11] with both articles intended to be part of a series on contemporary American artists "who have established themselves as masters." [12]

Lanman's enthusiasm for art deepened during his New York years when he began to frequent the auction houses and come to know the art dealers. An innovative art critic, he went beyond the exhibitions to become better informed about the artists and their work by visiting their studios. After he left New York in 1845, he kept up an active correspondence with many of them, ostensibly with future publication in mind; on a broader level it reflected his continuing support of American art in general and a genuine concern for the welfare and patronage of the younger artists. He enjoyed a particularly close personal relationship with the reclusive William Sidney Mount, whose reputation was already established, and at the same time maintained close friendships with less fortunate painters like the minister-artist Johannes Oertel and William Rowzee. As a result of his later travels, his circle of artist friends included Seth Eastman, John Mix Stanley, and William T. Ranney, whose productions documented scenery and life on the frontier.

An exceptionally able draftsman himself, Lanman developed a passion for collecting drawings and watercolors as well as paintings by his contemporaries. The chance discovery, some twenty-five years ago, of his collection of drawings, comprising about one hundred sheets dating from about 1837 to 1884, included representative examples by fifty-five American and foreign artists, all carefully labeled and mounted in an album. As a unit, the collection clearly identifies Lanman as the earliest known collector systematically to organize a selection of American drawings with a sense of purpose and direction.

From very early in his collecting career he seems to have been aware of the potential intrinsic value of his holdings. In 1842, when the twenty-three-year-old junior clerk suddenly found himself short of funds, he attempted to sell his collection to Carey & Lea, the Philadelphia publishers of gift books and literary annuals,[13] displaying a considerable knowledge of current values. He also unquestionably had its worth uppermost in mind when shortly thereafter he consigned the collection to a shrewd New York dealer of his acquaintance. It was only after one of the artists in his album, William Sidney Mount, learned by chance about his intention, and promptly sent him a stinging reprimand,[14] that Lanman tried to retrieve the drawings. Since his claim to the collection apparently remained unresolved for some time, several of the more important sheets, including those by Morse, Durand, Inman, Chapman, and Doughty, seem to have been dispersed. When ultimately reclaimed, the core of the early collection still contained significant drawings by William and Shepard Mount, Cole, Huntington, and Flagg among the Americans, and by English artists Eastlake, Abraham Cooper, Harvey, and Chinnery. The later collection chiefly reflected additions made after 1845, but the later additions never quite matched the quality of those earlier missing names.

In 1842, when it was unusual for a collector to make loans of this kind, Lanman elected to send a drawing by William Apthorp Adams and a watercolor by John Gadsby Chapman to the National Academy exhibition.[15] Described as from the "Sketch-book of an Amateur," the loans seem to have been calculated to attract public notice to the graphic accomplishments of the artists, although they undoubtedly also drew attention to the young collector. In later years, Lanman apparently encouraged such recognition when his "collection of original studies" was described in *The Crayon* as "most unique and valuable."[16] We know that he welcomed visitors to his Georgetown home to see the drawings and the "fine cabinet collection" of paintings by contemporary American and European artists he had assembled by the 1850s.

My collection includes forty drawings and watercolors from the Lanman Album, among them the drawing by Adams he lent to the early Academy show. For this exhibition a necessarily limited selection has been made but it does include Daniel Huntington's portrait of Lanman (Cat. No. 17), dating from his earliest collecting years, George Whiting Flagg's study of a young woman ("Marguerite") (Cat. No. 10), and Johannes A. S. Oertel's "Portrait of an Elderly Man" (Cat. No. 27).

John Mackie Falconer (1820-1903), Lanman's junior by a year, formed a collection of drawings and watercolors by American and some foreign artists after he settled in New York in 1848. His "Album" of sixty drawings (now in the Karolik Collection of the Museum of Fine Arts, Boston) includes the works of at least twenty-two artists and appears to represent more a friendship album than a formal collection. Falconer's wide acquaintance with his fellow artists is reflected in the many examples by his close friend Cropsey, along with single sheets by a variety of both professional and amateur artists, among them Lanman and William A. Adams.

Falconer was himself a capable painter in oil and watercolor (Cat. No. 9) who exhibited his work regularly at the National Academy for about forty years. Like Lanman, he began to collect the work of his contemporaries while he was still a youth. Although we know that he treasured an extremely rare drawing by Gilbert Stuart, drawings seem to have held only a peripheral interest for him. He focused his attention chiefly on building the fine collection of American and European pictures from which he made selective loans to Academy shows during the 1840s and 1850s. He evidently continued to add to the collection as late as 1863 when he acquired Thomas Cole's masterpiece, *Titan's Goblet* (Metropolitan Museum of Art).[17]

In 1867, when Tuckerman described James C. McGuire's collection of American paintings in some detail, he also noted that the Washington collector had also assembled some three hundred drawings to complement pictures by many of the same artists.[18] The collection was dispersed at auction in 1888,[19] but drawings have turned up by Bingham, Doughty, Edmonds, Durand, Agate, as well as Lanman (a Washington neighbor), all of which can be identified as part of the original McGuire holdings.

Attempts such as these to form concentrated collections of American drawings did not come about again until the early decades of the present century when a few teaching Institutions, notably the Carnegie Institute, Pittsburgh, The Cooper Union, New York, Phillips Academy, Andover, Massachusetts, and Princeton University, saw the opportunity to develop substantial study collections. While the histories of those collections all provide fascinating reading, Princeton's holds particular interest since its inception is due entirely to the efforts of a scholar-collector, Frank Jewett Mather, Jr., whose personal holdings are the centerpiece of the university collection. Mather, a professor of art history at Princeton and director of its museum for twenty-four years, was a noted Renaissance scholar who also wrote extensively on American art. Beginning in the late 1920s, and continuing until the 1940s, he gradually built a private collection devoted to American drawings that focused more on the highlights of draftsmanship than on a chronological history. His eye for quality is evident particularly in the drawings he acquired by Cole, Homer, La Farge, Eastman Johnson, and William Morris Hunt.[20]

By far the most ambitious project in the field originated with Maxim Karolik of Newport, whose great enthusiasm for American art extended to Colonial and Early Federal furniture and painting of the first three-quarters of the nineteenth century, as well as to drawings and watercolors of that period. Destined for Boston's Museum of Fine Arts, Karolik's contract with the museum in 1935 proposed an acquisition program in the three areas of painting, furniture, and drawings which was to evolve over some twenty-seven years. The drawing section, which ultimately encompassed some three thousand sheets, was assembled in close collaboration with the museum's curator of prints, Henry P. Rossiter. As a comprehensive survey that ranged from academic to folk artists, with sections devoted to "visiting foreign artists" and Civil War artist-reporters, the collection was designed primarily as a study resource. The size and scope of the material make it invaluable for the cultural historian; however, the obvious variations in quality when collecting on such a vast scale are counterbalanced by the insights provided for the would-be connoisseur into the character of American draftsmanship in the nineteenth century.[21]

In recent years, the interest in American drawings has grown considerably, but with a concentration almost universally on work after 1940, and by contemporary artists who have brought drawing into the mainstream of their production. The public has become accustomed to seeing drawings exhibited beside paintings as independent works of art, and has responded by readily acquiring them at commensurably substantial prices. The still relatively few collectors of American "old masters" tend to keep a much lower profile while they compete with one another, and with some major museums, for the rarer important drawings that periodically turn up in the art market. Not very long ago, the National Gallery of Art, Washington, acquired the greater part of the holdings of a long-time collector, John Davis Hatch, Jr.,[22] to fill an obvious gap in its collections. Dedicated private collectors like

Paul Magriel,[23] Stuart P. Feld, and others, including myself, attempt to assemble drawings of historical and esthetic significance in an area of scholarship and expertise that is still relatively undeveloped in this country, and almost unknown abroad.

It was indeed the possibility of further investigation in an unexplored field that first attracted me to American drawings when I was a graduate student of art history in New York. It was deepened during the six years I served as Keeper of Drawings and Prints at The Cooper Union Museum, where the collections included major holdings of drawings by Homer, Huntington, Frederic E. Church, and Thomas Moran which had been acquired, through the foresight of the museum's founders, by gift from the artists or their descendants. Although there had been no further encouragement or ready funding available in subsequent years to develop a more comprehensive collection, it was still possible in the early 1950s to persuade similar donations to the museum of the work of William T. Richards, Elihu Vedder, and Jerome Myers, as well as Scribner's collection of American illustrators.

The idea of forming a personal research collection had its beginnings about the time I curated an exhibition *American Impressions: Over 150 Years of Life and Humour in American Drawings and Watercolours* which, under other related titles, was held in New York, London, Rouen, and Munich, in 1954.[24] This show of over 130 drawings selected from numerous public and private collections, and sponsored by the United States Information Agency, was the first of its kind to travel extensively abroad.

Although opportunities to acquire representative material at modest cost were still good, my purpose was to develop a collection of quality which would not only reflect personal preference and reflection, but also demonstrate with historical balance the many varied aspects and phases of American draftsmanship. I was equally interested in exploring the idea of drawings as a visual experience, specifically in terms of instruction, kinds of drawings, and how they were used once artists began to recognize practical and esthetic values of the medium. This also included awareness of techniques and materials which are so often important indications of the evolution of an artistic tradition. A positive result of this investigation was the discovery that one self-taught draftsman, George Caleb Bingham, was in all probability the first American painter to follow Renaissance tradition by making use of cartoon drawings in the preparation of his narrative pictures.[25]

Drawings that reflect the creative process in the early preparation of a work of art usually consist of rapid first sketches, studies from nature, or document time and place, and they have the immediacy of an autograph that has always made a profound impression on me. The drawings in the collection by Morse (Cat. No. 22), Greenough (Cat. No. 11), Sully (Cat. No. 36), and William Sidney Mount (Cat. No. 23), are typical examples that not only reveal a selective taste but, more important, an intimate glimpse of the private world of an artist.

The in-depth acquisition of some twenty-five drawings by Benjamin West, whose legacy in the medium documents a prodigious lifetime production in all techniques and materials ranging from summary sketches to highly finished compositions, was an inevitable outgrowth of this special area of investigation on my part. This carefully chosen series of drawings provides not only an understanding of West's working method, but also a deeper insight into the life and times, and artistic character, of the first of America's great draftsmen (Cat. No. 42).

As a whole, the collection tends to adhere to a now familiar pattern in American art history in showing the evolution of portrait, figure, landscape, history, and genre from the late eighteenth century to about 1940. It also includes the development of illustration and caricature in which emphasis is given particularly to the role of the artist-correspondent of the American wars, and several aspects of the social scene.

Faces and Figures attempts to encompass, with a chronological parameter in mind, a development that displays not only formalistic change but also the contributory role drawings have assumed in an evolving American art history during the past century and more. The present exhibition of slightly over forty drawings and watercolors, the first of three projected for special exhibition at the Huntington, represents only a very small selection of the larger collection I have assembled over the past thirty-five years.

E. Maurice Bloch

NOTES

1. Dunlap, William, *History of the Rise and Progress of the Arts of Design in the United States*, New York, George P. Scott & Co., 1834, v. II, pp. 459-461.
2. Constable, William G., *Art Collecting in the United States of America: The Outline of a History*, London, Thomas Nelson, Ltd. [1964].
3. Cummings, Thomas Seir, *Historic Annals of the National Academy of Design, New York Drawing Association*, etc. . . . , Philadelphia, George W. Childs, 1865, pp. 21-29.
4. Cowdrey, Mary Bartlett (comp.), *National Academy Record, 1826-1860*, New York, Printed for the New-York Historical Society, 1943, 2v. The pattern was familiar. Drawings and watercolors were shown at the older Pennsylvania Academy of the Fine Arts as early as 1811, in its first exhibition, and at the Artists' Fund Society from its founding in 1835.
5. Cummings, *Historic Annals* . . . , pp. 110-112; John Durand, *Life and Times of A.B. Durand*, New York, Charles Scribner's Sons, 1894, pp. 90-97.
6. An interesting, detailed account of the non-artistic activities of The Sketch Club is given by James T. Callow, *Kindred Spirits: Knickerbocker Writers and American Artists, 1807-1855*, Chapel Hill, University of North Carolina Press, [1967], pp. 12-29. The predominantly social character of the meetings, in which conviviality was heightened by generous liquid refreshment, stimulated witty conversation and lively discourse on a wide range of topics, but discouraged the practice of drawing.
7. The Century (The Century Association), an exclusive social organization composed of authors, artists, and "amateurs of letters and the fine arts" evolved from The Sketch Club in 1846.
8. Cummings reappears in connection with sketch club activities in a group of four drawings by Durand, Chapman, Edmonds, and Alfred Jones (M. & M. Karolik Collection, Museum of Fine Arts, Boston), which apparently relate to The Artists' Sketching Club, and can be dated between 1844 and 1846. They are inscribed to Cummings who may have hosted or monitored the session and supplied the intriguing topic, "Raising the Wind." A more important group of nine sketches is inscribed to Cole (Karolik Collection), and evidently originated with the same club during the same period. The artists of this group of sketches includes Cummings among the participants, along with other familiar sketch club artists Durand, Cole, Ingham, Edmonds, Gray, John L. Morton, and J.H. Shegogue. The topic of the one-hour session was "The Trying Hour," its ambiguous interpretation hopefully appreciated by the participants. Cole was one of the founders of The Artists' Sketching Club in 1844.
9. Stebbins, Theodore E., *American Master Drawings and Watercolors: A History of Works on Paper from Colonial Times to the Present*,

New York, Harper & Row, [1976], pp. 113-114.

10. *U.S. Democratic Review,* III, June, 1843, pp. 598-603.

11. *The New World,* VIII (6), February 10, 1844, pp. 185-188.

12. The story of Lanman's life and career after he left New York in 1845 is remarkable itself. Although he continued to send pictures to the annual National Academy shows on a more or less regular basis for many years afterward, he recognized his amateur status and tended more to use his artistic talent to record his extensive travels to still unexplored regions of the country. He became, in succession, a newspaper editor, librarian of the War Department, private secretary to Daniel Webster, librarian of the Interior Department and the House of Representatives, and the first American Secretary of the Japanese Legation. An author of several books on travel, biography, and the science of angling, his most noteworthy writings on art besides criticism were a series of perceptive biographical essays about artists he knew personally, some of which he published in *Haphazard Personalities: Chiefly of Noted Americans . . . ,* Boston and New York, 1886.

13. Lanman to Carey & Lea, New York, November 8, 1842 (New York Public Library). Henry C. and Edward L. Carey, the Philadelphia publishers, were also well-known patrons and collectors of American art.

14. W.S. Mount to Lanman, Stony Brook, L.I., May 20, 1843 (New-York Historical Society)

15. *National Academy Exhibition Record,* I, pp. 3, 76.

16. *The Crayon,* I, February 28, 1855, 137.

17. Anderson Auction Co., New York, April 28, 1904, Sale no. 299, *John M. Falconer (Brooklyn), Oil Paintings, Water Colors & Engravings.*

18. Tuckerman, Henry Theodore, *Book of the Artists, American Artist Life . . . ,* New York, G.P. Putman & Son, 1867, p. 632.

19. Thomas Dowling, Washington, D.C., *Catalogue of the Collection of Paintings, Statuary, Bronzes &c. Belonging to the Estate of the Late J.C. McGuire, to be Sold by Order of His Executors on December 10th* [1888], *& Following Days . . . ,* [Washington, D.C., 1888].

20. Princeton, N.J., The Art Museum, Princeton University, *American Drawings in the Art Museum, Princeton University,* by Barbara T. Ross. [Exhibition October 3-November 28, 1976] [Princeton, N. J., 1976].

21. Boston, Massachusetts, Museum of Fine Arts, *M. & M. Karolik Collection of American Water Colors & Drawings,* Introduction by Henry P. Rossiter. [Exhibition October 18, 1962-January 6, 1963] Boston, Mass., Museum of Fine Arts, 1962, 2v.

22. Selections from the Hatch collection have been shown in this country since 1937 and one hundred drawings were chosen for exhibitions held in England, Ireland, and France in 1976-1977.

23. The Magriel collections have been exhibited widely in this country since the early 1960s, notably in shows held from 1964-1967 and 1979-1981.

24. New York, The Cooper Union Museum, *An Exhibition of American Drawings, Assembled for the United States Information Agency by the Smithsonian Institution Traveling Exhibition Service,* January 29-March 6, 1954.
Munich, Amerika Hauses, *Amerikanische Zeichnungen aus Zwei Jahrhunderten* [Exhibition] 1954.
Rouen, Musée des Beaux Arts, *Dessin Américain au XVIIIe Siècle à Nos Jours* [Exhibition] 19 juin-18 juillet [1954].
London, London Tea Centre, *American Impressions: Over 150 Years of Life and Humor in Drawings and Watercolours* [Exhibition] 6-21 August, 1954. Introduction by E. Maurice Bloch.

25. Bloch, E. Maurice, *The Drawings of George Caleb Bingham. With a Catalogue Raisonné,* Columbia, Mo., University of Missouri Press, 1975.

FACES AND FIGURES IN AMERICAN DRAWINGS

NO. 1 ESTHER FRANCES (FRANCESCA) ALEXANDER (1837-1917)

Design for "Life of Saint Zita"
Pen and bistre ink on paper watermarked WHATMAN; 15 1/4 x 11 in.

Lit: Roadside Songs of Tuscany, Translated and Illustrated by Francesca Alexander and Edited by John Ruskin, Orpington, 1885, Plate IV; *Tuscan Songs Collected, Translated, and Illustrated by Francesca Alexander* [Boston, 1897], Plate LXXVII.

Prov: The artist, Florence (Italy); John Ruskin; Sven M.A. Bruntjen, Woodside, California.

The final design for the plate in the series of illustrations of the songs and hymns of the Tuscan Contadini assembled by Francesca Alexander during the many years she resided in the region. For the *Roadside Songs of Tuscany* she made a selection of the songs, translated them into English, and illustrated them with her own drawings. The drawings were probably produced between 1868 and 1882. Her plan was to sell the manuscript and distribute the proceeds of the sale to the poor. John Ruskin, who had learned about Alexander from Henry Roderick Newman, a mutual acquaintance, visited her in Florence in 1882. When he saw her *Roadside Songs* he was so impressed that he immediately purchased the entire manuscript of 122 leaves for £600. Ruskin ultimately donated about two-thirds of it to the Sheffield Museum, to Oxford and Cambridge Universities, gave a few sheets to friends, and retained the rest for his personal collection at Brantwood. The present sheet was among the 50 drawings originally in Ruskin's own collection.

After Ruskin returned to England and Oxford in 1882, he included Alexander in his lectures; at a private lecture in London in 1883, he displayed some twenty of the illustrations to *Roadside Songs.* Ruskin was taken by Alexander's sensitive line and ideal concept of form which, for the critic, seemed to embody the visual and moral values he required of art at the time. In writing of *Roadside Songs*, he said "In absolute skill of drawing and perception of all that is loveliest in human creatures—and in the flowers that live for them—I think these works are in their kind unrivalled, and that they do indeed represent certain elements of feeling and power peculiar to this age. . . ."

Francesca Alexander was born in Boston, the daughter of the well-known portrait painter Francis Alexander (1800-1880), who had settled in the city about 1827. She started to sketch as a child, and evidently received some instruction from her father, but was mainly self-trained in developing drawing as an important means of self-expression. The family visited Italy from 1831 to 1833, then returned to Boston until 1853, when they decided to make Florence their permanent home. In Florence they occupied two floors of the Hotel Bonciani, overlooking the Piazza Santa Novella. From her studio located on the top floor, Francesca made most of the drawings of flowers, views of local scenery, and of Tuscan life she incorporated into her illustrations of *Roadside Songs.* A deeply religious woman, she led a reclusive life, and never married. Although she remained in Florence for the remainder of her life, she always considered herself an American artist and writer.

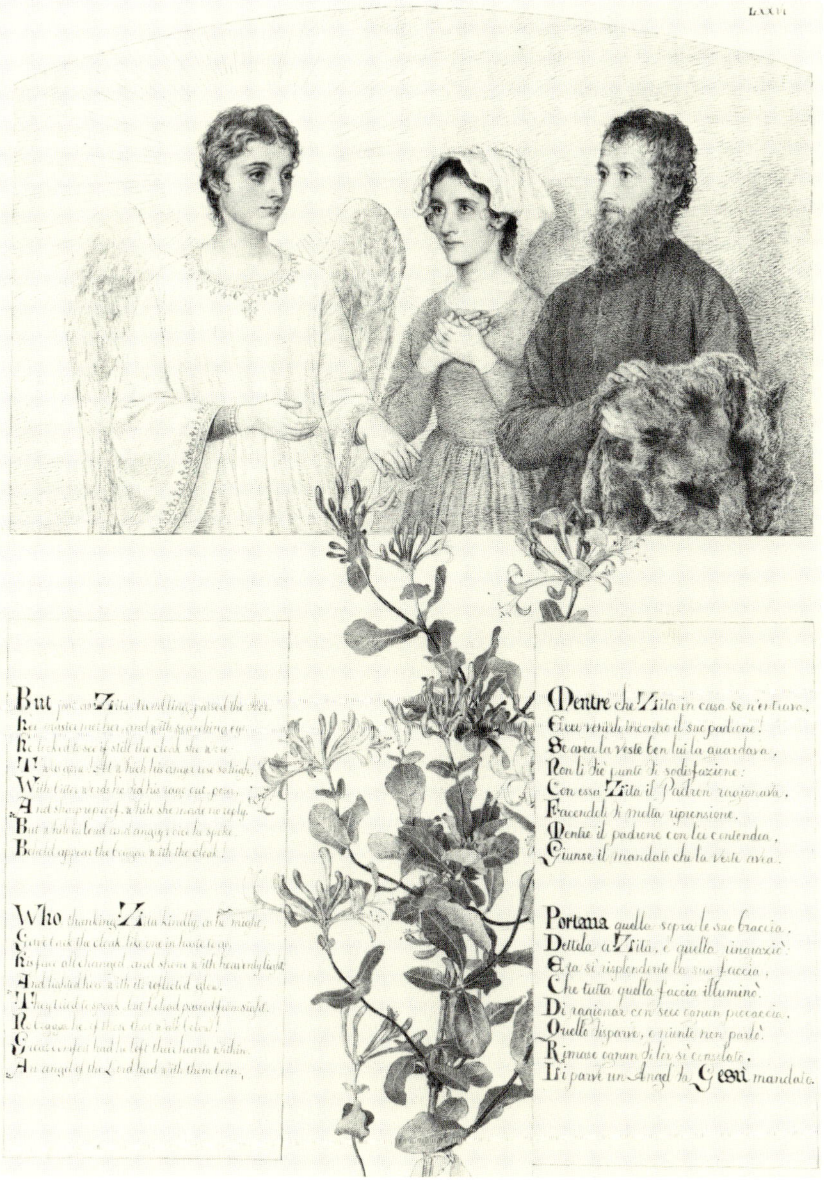
LXXII
With bitter words he did his rage out pour,
And sharp reproof, while she made no reply.
His face all changed and shone with heavenly light,
And bathed her with its reflected glow.
They tried to speak but he had passed from sight.
An angel of the Lord had with them been,
Mentre che Zita in casa se n'entrava,
Con essa Zita il Padron ragionava,
Mentre il padrone con lei contendea,
Portava quella sopra le sue braccia.
Che tutta quella faccia illuminò.
Li parve un Angel da Gesù mandato.

NO. 2 MATHER BROWN (1761-1831)

A Sailor on Shore-leave, ca. 1812
Pen and brown ink, heightened with white, on brown paper; 5 x 7³/₈ in.

Signed lower right: M. Brown

Brown was born in Boston of a distinguished New England family that could claim descent from John Cotton, Cotton Mather, and Increase Mather. His precocious artistic talent was already recognized by his early teens when he was encouraged to write and publish verse, receive some drawing lessons from Gilbert Stuart, and take on commissions to paint miniatures. At sixteen he was an itinerant portrait and miniature painter in New England, New York, and the West Indies. By 1780 he had set aside enough to go abroad to study, expecting to increase his prospects by studying to become a history painter. Armed with a letter of introduction to Benjamin Franklin, then in Versailles, who welcomed him and in turn provided him with an introduction to Benjamin West, Brown arrived in London in 1781. West readily admitted him to his studio as a pupil. By coincidence, Gilbert Stuart was also in residence in the studio at the time. Although Brown seems to have received some supervisory training in painting technique from Stuart, he was deeply inspired by West's example and sought to emulate the master's unprecedented accomplishment as an American artist abroad. In 1784 he was admitted to the Royal Academy for further training, only the second American to be so honored. For a time Brown's prospects for early success in London art and social circles seemed exceptionally bright. He began to exhibit at the Royal Academy, the British Institution, and elsewhere. By 1788 he earned a considerable reputation in England and America and received numerous commissions for portraits. Unfortunately, his success was to be short-lived and, in 1810, he found it necessary to leave the city to eke out a livelihood in the provinces. He taught painting in Buckinghamshire and, once again an itinerant, painted portraits in Bath, Bristol, Staffordshire, and finally Lancashire, chiefly in Manchester and Liverpool, where he was to remain some thirteen years. He afterward returned to London and spent his last years there in obscurity. Since Brown planned to follow in West's footsteps as a history and religious painter, the drawings and studies he produced in West's studio show a decided influence of the master's subject matter, composition, and drawing style. This drawing, like a number of others that date from his late years as an independent artist, reflect a more personal observation of everyday life, often with a touch of satire. The sketches of the Liverpool period, to which this drawing probably belongs, are highly individual and particularly broad in style and technique.

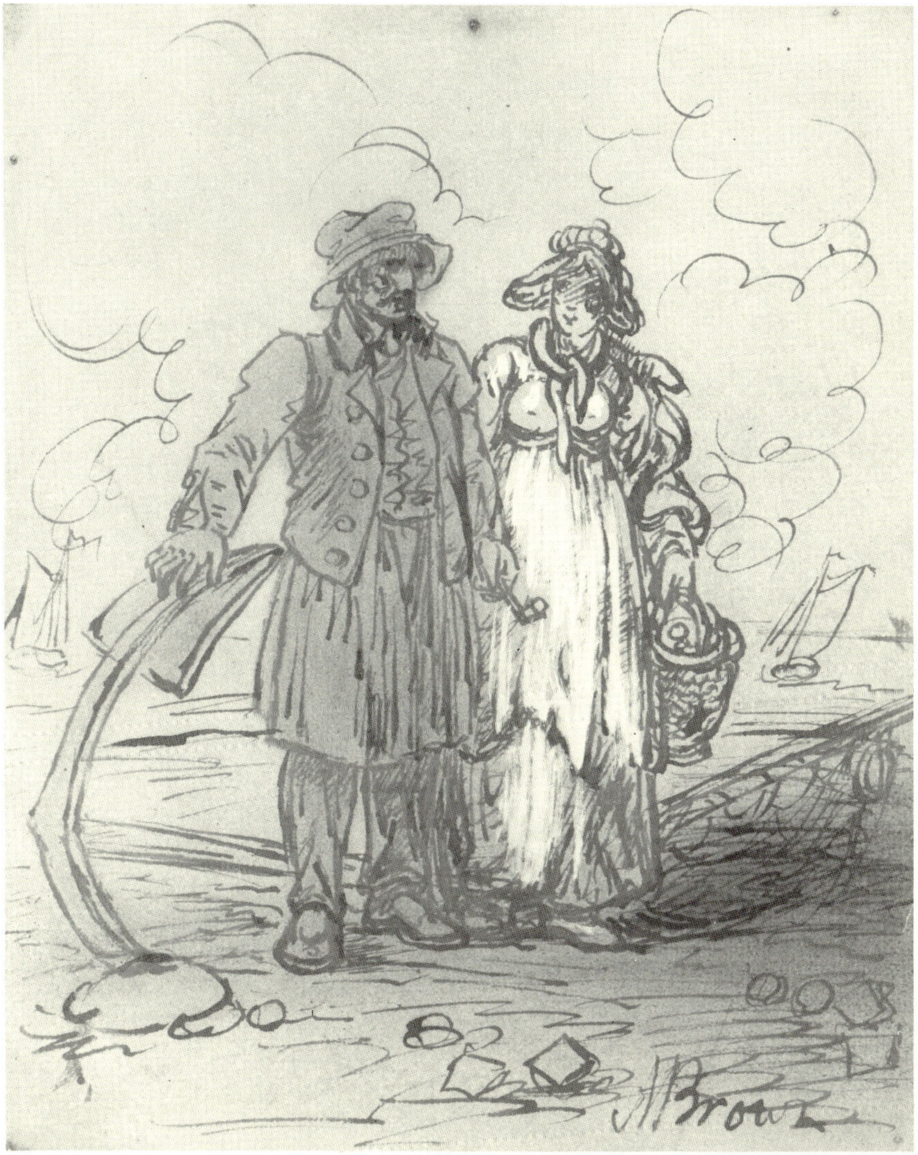
J. Brown

NO. 3 WILLIAM MERRITT CHASE (1849-1916)

An Infanta, Souvenir of Velasquez
Pen and ink on tan paper; 7 3/8 x 11 1/8 in.

Signed and inscribed upper right; Velasquez/by/Wm. M. Chase.

Chase was born in a small town south of Indianapolis, the son of a well-to-do drygoods merchant who later moved the family home and business to Indianapolis. He showed an early talent for art that led to some lessons from a local painter before he was sent to New York for some formal study with Joseph Oriel Eaton, and at the National Academy with Lemuel E. Wilmarth who had been trained in Munich and Paris. In 1871 he went to St. Louis, where his family then resided, and while there, executed several pictures that inspired a group of patrons to finance a trip to Munich to further his studies at the Royal Academy. Chase's teachers there during the next four years included Alexander Wagner, Karl von Piloty, and Wilhelm Leibl. At the same time, close observation of the works of old masters like Van Dyck and Hals greatly influenced his independent studies. In 1877 he went to Venice in the company of fellow-students Frank Duveneck and John H. Twachtman. When he returned to New York in 1878, he settled in one of the Tenth Street Studios he later made famous both in his paintings and as center of his colorful social life. He also began his teaching career at that time.

His friends J. Carroll Beckwith and Robert Blum encouraged him to accompany them to France and Spain in 1881, an event that was to begin Chase's particular fascination with Spain and Velasquez. In New York, Chase became a most successful painter and teacher. He married, settled in Brooklyn for a time, then in New York. He afterward built a summer home at Shinnecock, Long Island. His teaching commitments in later years included the Brooklyn Art School, classes at the Studio, and at the Chase School he started in 1896. From 1897 on he took his students on summer tours abroad—Holland (1903), England (1904), Spain (1905), Italy (1911), and Belgium (1912)—and in 1914 he taught classes for the first time in California at Carmel. This drawing is a spontaneous sketch from memory which is more than likely a composite of Velasquez portraits in the Prado. Those portraits were evidently still much on his mind when he painted the portrait of his daughter Helen Velasquez Chase as "An Infanta" in 1899.

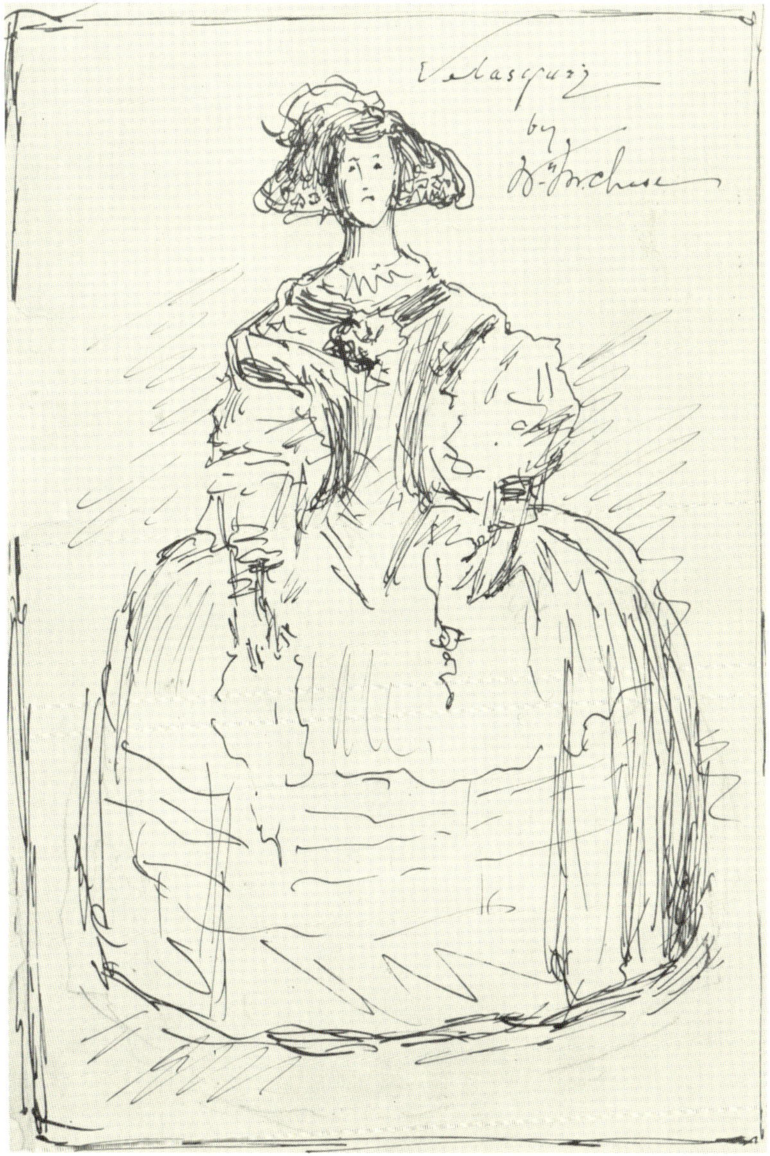
Velasquez
by
W. M. Chase

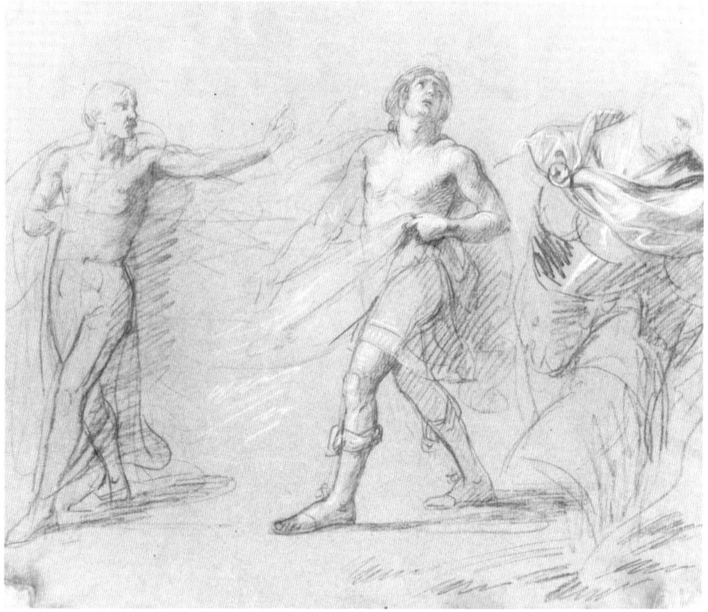

NO. 4 JOHN SINGLETON COPLEY (1738-1815)

Saul Reproved by Samuel for Not Obeying the Commandments of the Lord, 1797/1798
Black crayon and white chalk, on gray-blue paper; 13 x 14 1/2 in.

A double-sided sheet. Verso: Studies for the same subject, the central figures shown unclothed, with drapery details

Lit: Prown, J.D., *John Singleton Copley* (Cambridge, Massachusetts, Harvard University Press), 1966, II, pp. 351, 446, pls. 611, 613 (recto and verso identified as separate sheets)

Prov: Estate of the artist; John Singleton Copley, Jr. (1772-1863), later Lord Lyndhurst; probably in Lord Lyndhurst Library Sale, Christie's, London, Feb. 26-27, 1864, lot 669; sold to Dr. H. Albert Rosenthal, Philadelphia, Pennsylvania, 1935; Leo Dennis, Los Angeles, California, 1950.

Studies for the painting now in the collection of the Museum of Fine Arts, Boston. Completed in 1798, the picture was on exhibition the same year at the Royal Academy, London, no. 235, and at the British Institution, London, 1806, no. 63.

The subject is taken from 1 Samuel 15:27.

Copley produced eight recorded paintings of religious history during his residence in England, of which half were of subjects taken from the Old Testament. In this instance, the attraction that the particularly dramatic content this biblical source held for Copley also closely emulates Benjamin West's example, whose preference for the books of Samuel included at least three subjects painted before 1789, in addition to a number of drawings (see West, this catalogue).

Copley consistently made preparatory drawings for his paintings during his career in England, the most revealing being those he made for the history paintings he believed were so important to his career. The many drawings now extant which relate to

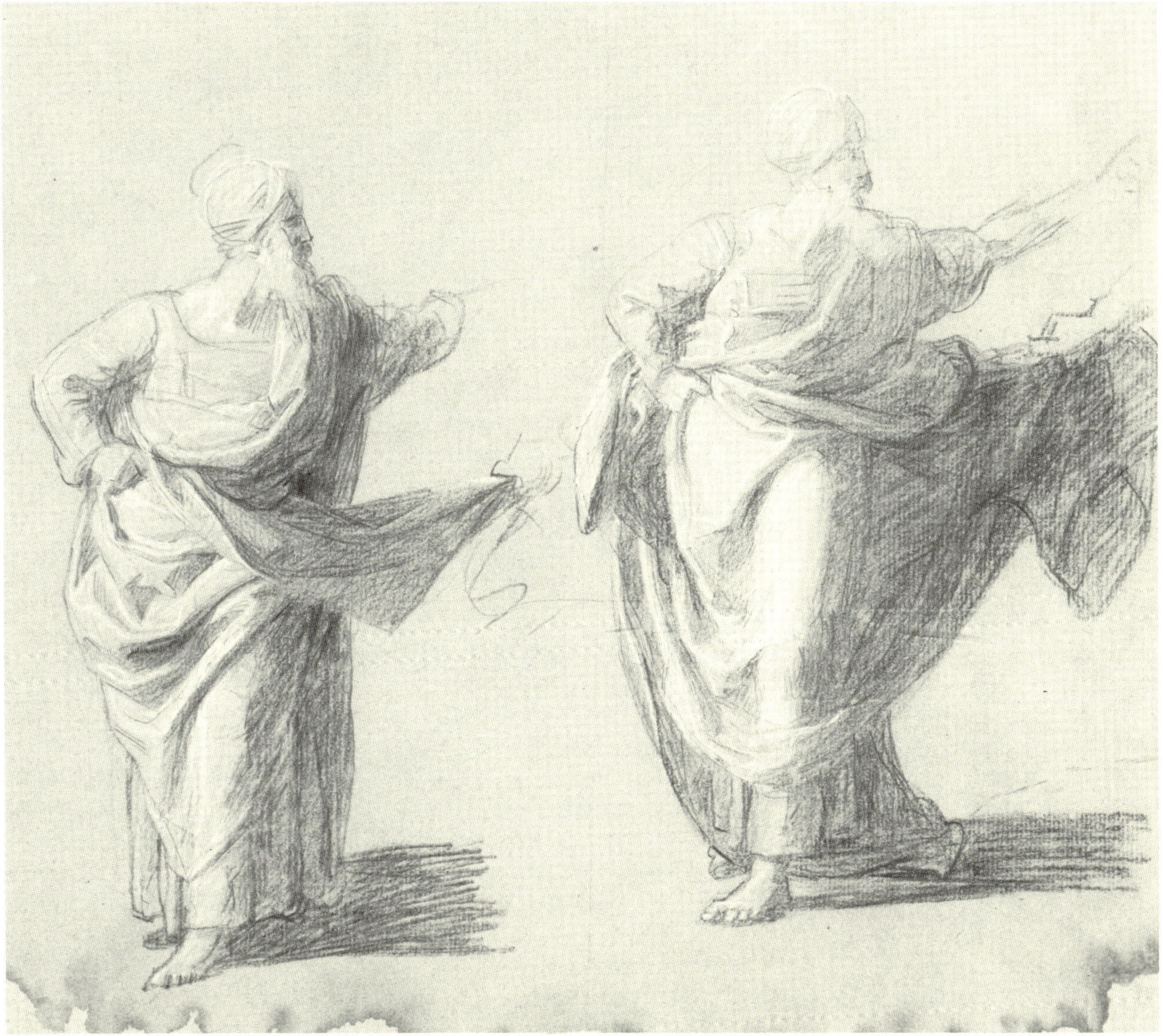

JOHN SINGLETON COPLEY

(Continued)

individual projects not only display his graphic style at its best but show the precise, progressive development of each picture from a general layout of the composition to the placement of each figure, gesture, and detail of costume. Both sides of this sheet display advanced progressive studies for the painting. The verso, which is probably the earlier of the two, shows the two central figures somewhat well advanced in concept, but still lacking the strong contraposto movement that gives the final composition its significance and dramatic effect. The figures of Samuel and Saul are studies in the nude and semi-nude, with an added detail of Saul's cape and hand. The disposition of the figures has been established, but the poses and gestures are still somewhat stilted and will be coordinated in the final version to emphasize the tension within the group. The obverse shows two variant studies of Samuel which are essentially details of the draped figure, probably made with the aid of a lay figure wrapped in wet cloths. Although neither describes the final solution, the whirling figure and outstretched arm of Samuel, as well as Saul's critical gesture described in verse 27—"Saul laid hold upon the skirt of his robe and rent it"—are already clearly defined.

NO. 5 KENYON COX (1856-1919)

Torso of "Hope" for* Hope and Memory, *1899

Pencil on cream paper; 21 1/4 x 16 in.

Signed lower right: K. Cox; inscribed below: "picture belonging to J.D. Cox - Cleveland"

A native of Ohio, Cox first studied at the McMicken School of Design in Cincinnati before going to the Pennsylvania Academy in Philadelphia in 1876. The following year he went to Paris, where he was a student in the ateliers of Carolus-Duran, Cabanel, and Gérome. His training in the prevailing French academic manner determined the traditional values he followed as a painter, illustrator, critic, and teacher in the years after his return to New York in 1882. As a teacher and critic he sought perfection in the classical sense and adopted strict rules of draftsmanship, anatomy, and proportion in his work. In *The Classic Point of View*, the series of Scammon lectures he gave in Chicago in 1911, Cox described the aims of drawing as "first, to develop in the highest degree the abstract beauty and significance possessed by lines in themselves, more or less independent of representation; second, to express with the utmost clearness and force the material significance of objects and especially, of the human body." In this example, his conception of drawing as dealing with "beauty and significance, not with mere fact," seems effectively demonstrated.

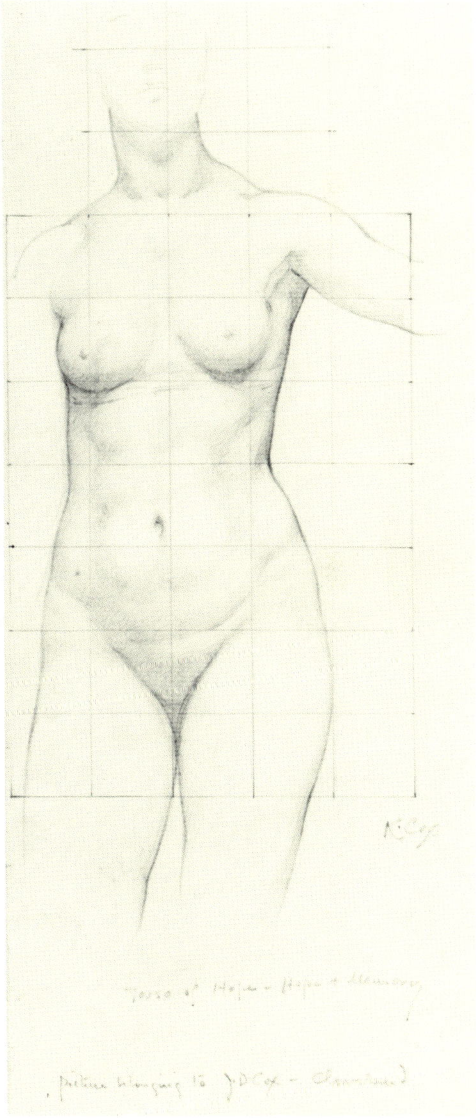

No. 6 Felix Octavius Carr Darley (1822-1888)

Portrait of Louis Lang, 1856
Pencil; 6 1/2 x 8 1/2 in.

Signed and dated, below: F. O. C. Darley - fecit -/56.

The subject, Louis Lang, established a reputation as a portrait, miniature, and genre painter. He was an Associate Member of the National Academy of Design in 1852, and a Member from 1853-1893. Born in Germany in 1814, he studied in Paris in 1834 before emigrating to America in 1838. After a residence in Philadelphia, he went to Italy for several years before returning to settle permanently in New York in 1847. He died in New York in 1893.

Darley's reputation as an artist was earned entirely by his drawings, chiefly those he produced as an illustrator for the greatest writers of the day, such as Fenimore Cooper, Washington Irving, Nathaniel Hawthorne, Henry Wadsworth Longfellow, Harriet Beecher Stowe, Francis Parkman, and Charles Dickens. Born in Philadelphia, he early displayed a remarkable talent for drawing that attracted the attention of Thomas Sully. Sully was instrumental in getting the Philadelphia publisher Henry C. Carey to recommend Darley to the New York publisher Appleton. Sully wrote directly to Appleton in 1842, "on the subject of some drawings by Mr. F. Darley, which I think worthy of your notice;—as the work of a young artist I think them wonderful." It is entirely possible that Carey and Sully's intervention on Darley's behalf succeeded that same year in obtaining a commission from the editor of the *Saturday Museum*, Edgar Allan Poe. Darley was to continue his association with Poe when, in 1843, two of his drawings were selected to illustrate "The Gold Bug" when it first appeared in *The Dollar Newspaper.*

Portraits are relatively rare in Darley's work, but this drawing amply demonstrates his prodigious talent as a draftsman—in this instance to capture the likeness of a friend and colleague. Another portrait of the same subject by Darley has long been in the collection of the Century Association in New York (crayon: 20 1/4 x 15 3/4 in.). The Century Association, which grew out of the Old Sketch Club, was founded in 1846. Lang was one of the artists admitted to its membership in 1849, and Darley the following year, most likely on Lang's recommendation.

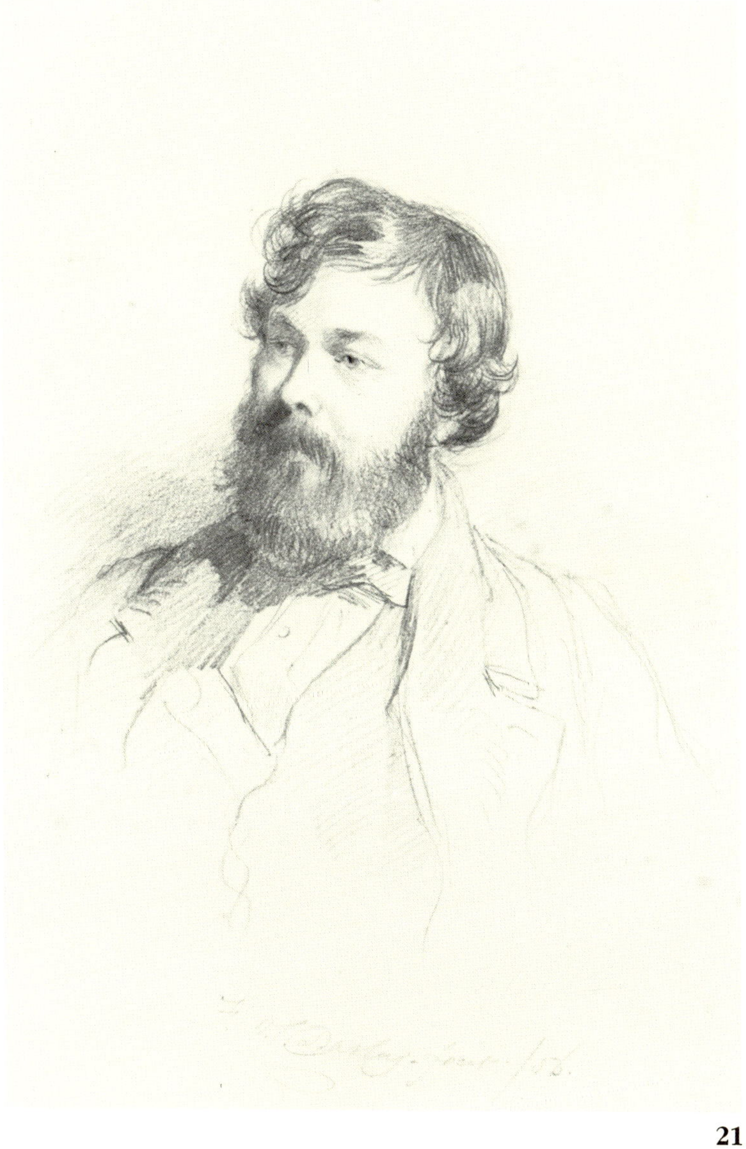

NO. 7 ARTHUR BOWEN DAVIES (1862-1928)

Two Standing Nudes
Pastel on tan paper ; $16^{7}/_{8}$ x $11^{1}/_{2}$ in.(sight)

Estate stamp signature, lower left, followed by initials in ink: V.M.D. [Dr. Virginia Meriwether Davies (1862-1949), widow of the artist].

Prov: Estate of the artist; Max Safron, New York.

Davies was born in Utica, New York, but moved to Chicago in his teens and received his first instruction in art there at the Chicago Academy of Design. In the early 1880s, following a stint as a draftsman for a civil engineering firm in Mexico City, he returned to Chicago for additional study at the Art Institute. By 1886 he was in New York, continuing his training at the Gotham Art Students School and the Art Students League. He supported himself by working as an illustrator for *St. Nicholas* and *Century* magazines. Davies traveled to Europe for the first time in 1893, where he became absorbed with the works of many of the old and then modern masters who were later to form the basis of his painting. Although his mature work reflects a diverse eclecticism that ranges from Botticelli to the English Pre-Raphaelites, as well as Puvis de Chavannes and Hans von Marées, he was as intuitively American as Ryder, a visionary who stood apart from the mainstream of the formal art world in this country at the time. A free spirit, he was a member of "The Eight" who exhibited at New York's Macbeth Gallery in 1908, and a leading force of the Armory Show of 1913. This drawing, which is probably a study for one of his paintings, is characteristic of the work of an artist who was a fastidious and sensitive craftsman. Whether it was a painting, a drawing, or an experimental graphic work, Davies always displayed an innate sense of linear rhythm and an emotional quality of color and texture that made a very personal artistic statement.

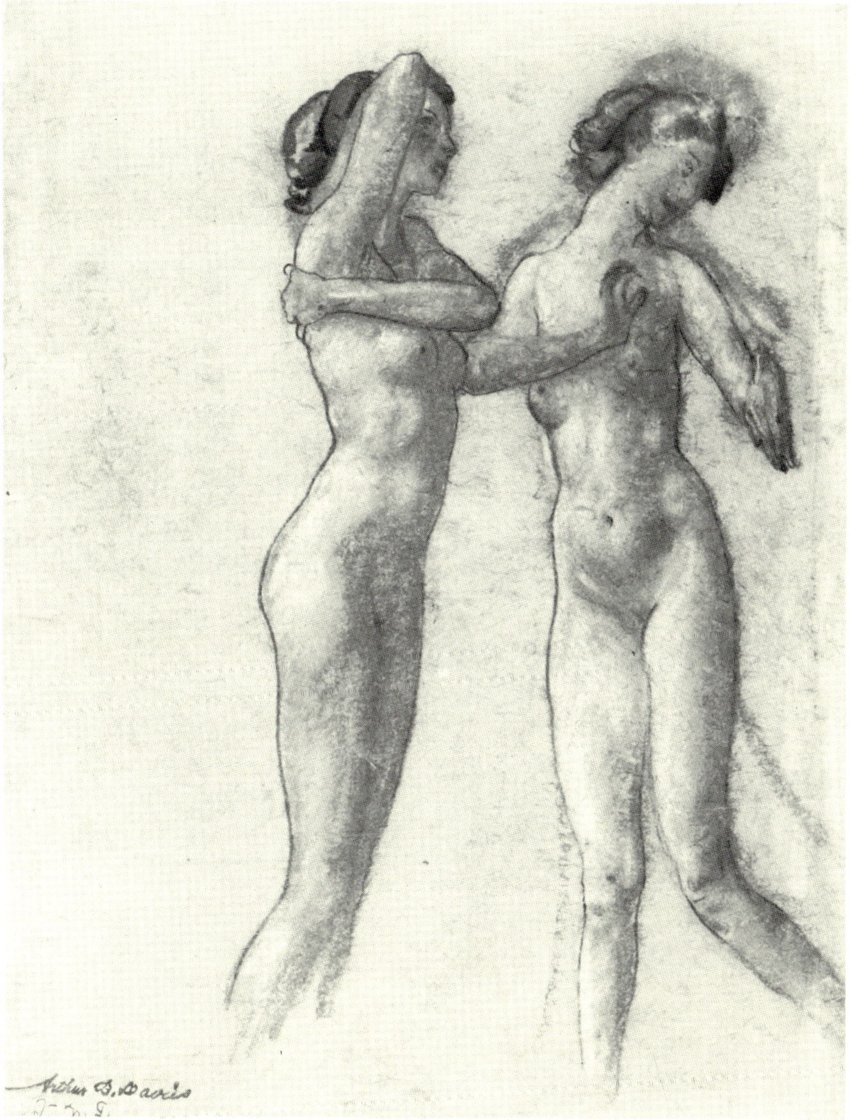
Arthur B. Davies

NO. 8 FRANK VINCENT DUMOND (1865-1951)

Study for the Figure of a Prophet, 1900
Charcoal on gray paper watermarked MICHALLET; 18 1/2 x 12 1/4 in.

Prov: Estate of the artist; wife, Helen Xavier DuMond; daughter Elizabeth DuMond Perry, Darien, Connecticut.

DuMond was born in Rochester, New York and began his studies at the Art Students League in 1884 with J. Carroll Beckwith and William Sartain. He afterward studied in Paris under Boulanger, Lefebvre, and Constant. During his early years in New York he supported himself as a newspaper illustrator for the *Daily Graphic* and *Harper's Weekly*. By the turn of the century, when he had already earned a reputation as a figure painter, DuMond continued to work for magazines like *Century*. The breadth of design and elegance of line he displayed in the illustrations of those later years prepared the way for the mural paintings for which he is perhaps best known. In 1892 DuMond started a distinguished career in teaching at the Art Students League, that lasted for fifty-nine years. At that time he exhibited at the National Academy, becoming an Associate Member in 1900, and a full Member in 1906. This drawing, which was most probably a preliminary study for the central figure in the headpiece illustration to "The Hymn" from John Milton's ode "On the Morning of Christ's Nativity," was published in *Century Magazine*, December, 1900.

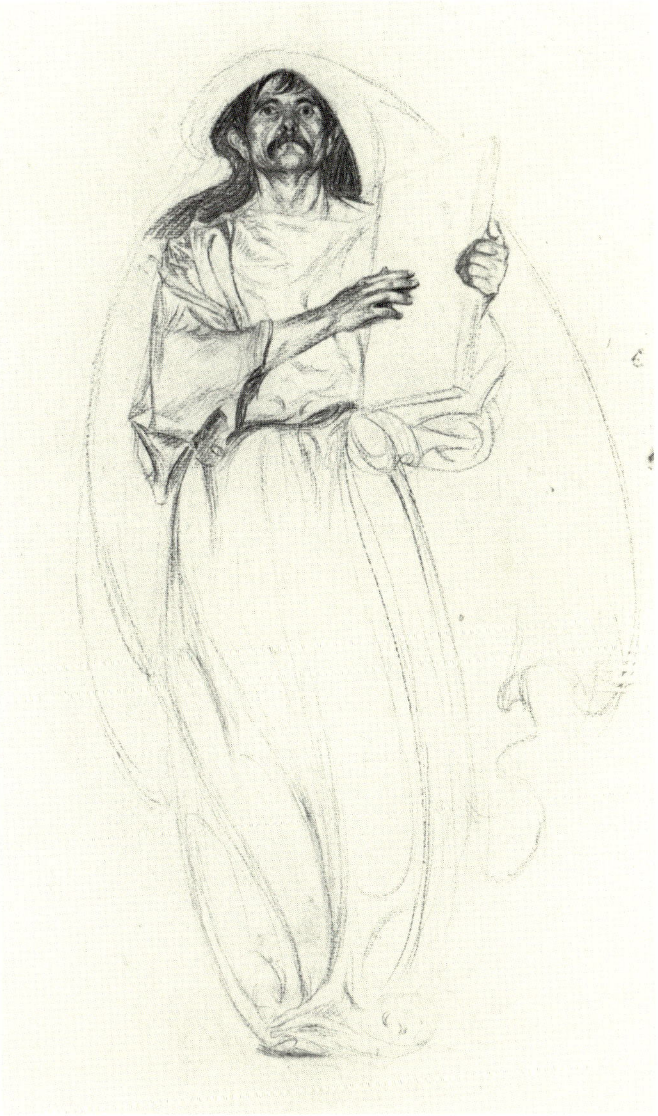

NO. 9 JOHN MACKIE FALCONER (1820-1903)

The Fruit Vendor, 1851
Watercolor and pencil on paper watermarked J. WHATMAN TURKEY MILL; 7 3/8 x 8 5/8 in.

Signed and dated lower right: J.M.F. Nov. 15/51.

Falconer was born in Scotland, came to America about 1836, settling in New York where he attended art classes at the National Academy and the Graham Art School in Brooklyn. He became a semi-professional artist who made his living in the more practical business world. Although he never earned more than an honorary membership at the National Academy, he exhibited regularly at the Academy for more than thirty years, as well as the Pennsylvania Academy of the Fine Arts and the Boston Athenaeum. An indefatigable draftsman, Falconer also worked in watercolor and oil and, in 1849, began to experiment with etching. He became especially active in the later 1860s and the 1870s when etching became a more popular art form here and abroad, and was one of the founding members of the New York Etching Club in 1877. Like another semi-professional artist of his time, Charles Lanman, he made sketching trips throughout the country and Canada and, again like Lanman, collected paintings and drawings by contemporary American and foreign artists. This drawing is from a large series of studies of street people Falconer made in New York in the 1850s. Several of the subjects, variously dated 1851, 1852, and 1856, are in the Karolik collection of American drawings at the Museum of Fine Arts in Boston.

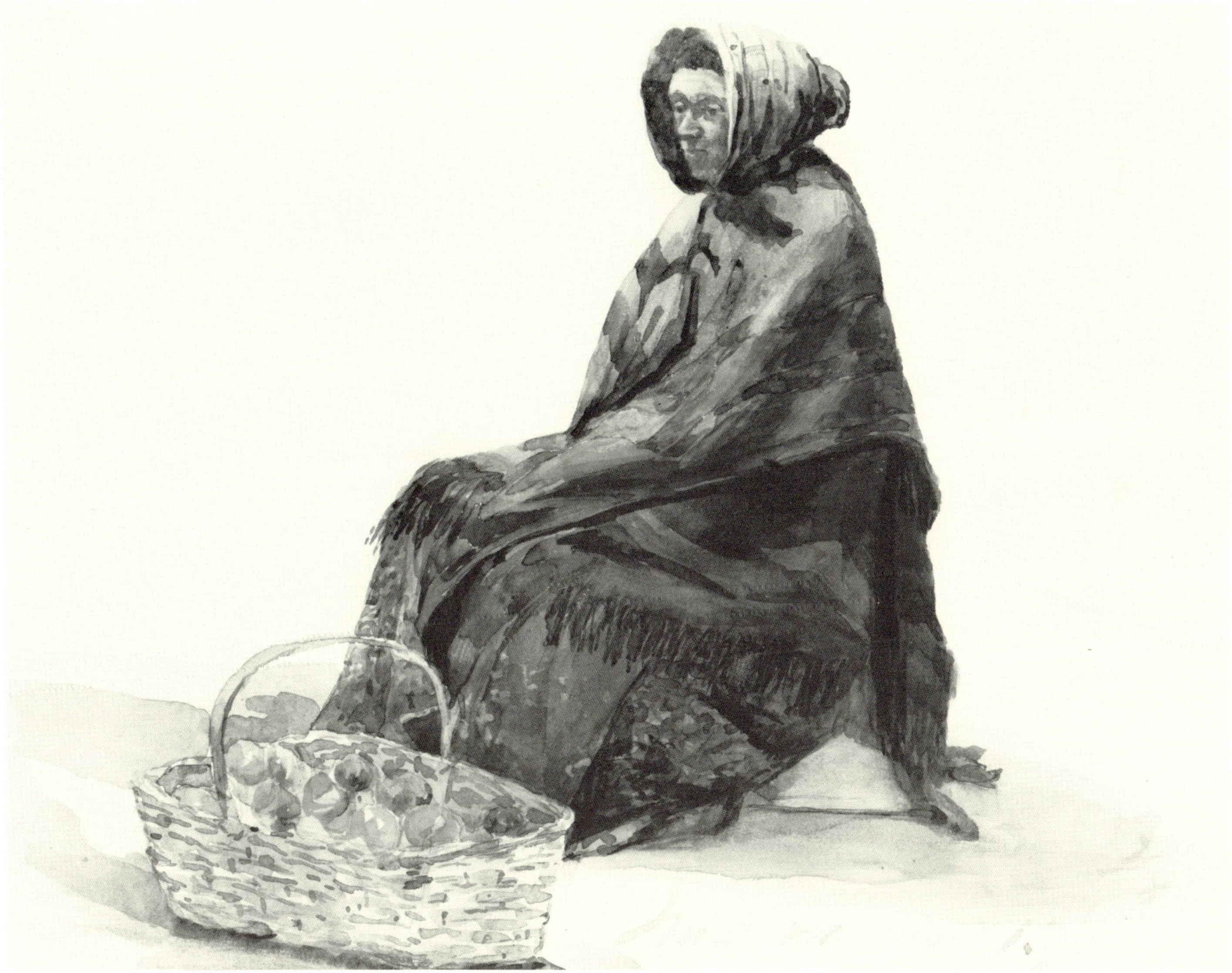

No. 10 George Whiting Flagg (1816-1897)

A Young Woman: Marguerite
Pencil on Bristol board; 11 1/2 x 9 1/8 in.

Inscribed: At lower right, in ink: G.W. Flagg (in Charles Lanman's hand)

Prov: The artist; presented to Charles Lanman, 1847.

Flagg was born in New Haven, Connecticut but was brought up in Charleston, South Carolina where he received his first instruction in painting. About 1833 he arrived in Boston to study for eighteen months with Washington Allston (Flagg's father was a half-brother of Allston) and an obscure portrait painter, James Bowman. Flagg was soon afterward sent to Europe by Luman Reed, the wealthy New York collector and patron of young American artists, where he was able to study the work of old masters in London, Paris, and Italy. On his return to the United States he worked in Boston and New York before settling in New York about 1843. He began to exhibit regularly at the National Academy from 1834 to 1867, and was elected to full membership of the Academy in 1851. This drawing provides a rare glimpse of the refinement and decorative manner that earned an early recognition of Flagg's figure painting. It was presented to the art critic Charles Lanman, who wrote an enthusiastic review of his painting *The Match Girl* for the *New York Express* in January 1847. It apparently stimulated an exchange of correspondence between the two men that led to Lanman's acquisition of the drawing.

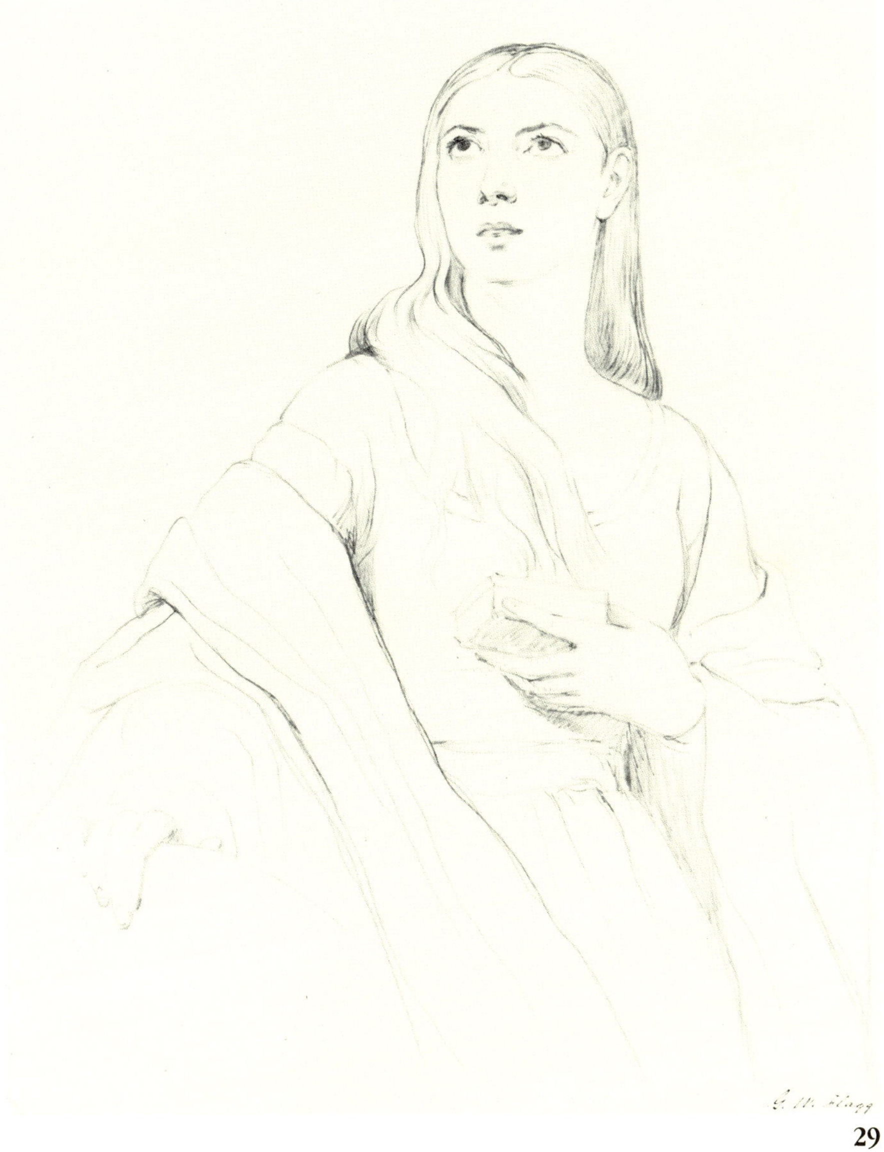

NO. 11 HORATIO GREENOUGH (1805-1852)

Sheet of Sketches, 1831
Sepia, pen and wash; 12 1/4 x 8 1/8 in.

We can date this historically significant documentary drawing precisely between mid-September and late November 1831 when Greenough arrived in Paris in the hope of modeling a bust of Lafayette, joining Samuel F. B. Morse and James Fenimore Cooper who were also in Paris at that time. The sheet is endorsed on the verso by Morse: "Sketches by Greenough one evening when we were in Paris together rue de Surenne No. 25" (Greenough and Morse were sharing rooms at that address within ten days of his arrival in Paris on September 6th). The silhouette sketches include Greenough himself, Morse, Lafayette, Cooper and his daughter, as well as George Washington, John Adams, Voltaire, and Napoleon, and also classical statues of the Venus de'Medici, Laocoön, and the Apollo Belvedere, all identified in pencil by Morse. Apart from Lafayette, Greenough modeled bust portraits of Morse and Cooper during his stay in Paris in the fall and winter of 1831.

Greenough showed an early talent for sculpture during his youth in Boston, but he and his family realized that a professional career for an American sculptor was almost without precedent at home. After completing a formal education at Harvard, he went abroad to study, settling in Rome for two years. Illness compelled him to return to the United States in 1827. In New York, early in the following year, he met Morse, then at the height of his artistic career in painting and founding-president of the National Academy of Design. They evidently became close friends from the start. Greenough was soon elected an Honorary Member of the Academy and afterward exhibited there from 1832-35, in 1841, and in 1848. When Greenough returned to Italy in 1828, he made Florence his headquarters for the following two decades. All his professional success during that time was due to the support of an American clientele which culminated in 1832 and 1837 with the two coveted commissions he received from the United States Congress, one for a colossal statue of Washington, the other for one of the groups of the East front of the Capitol. James Fenimore Cooper, the novelist, was a strong and influential supporter of his early efforts. Greenough met him in Florence in the late fall or early winter of 1828, and soon thereafter became an intimate friend of the family. He modeled a bust of Cooper, who then commissioned him to execute a marble group which Greenough's biographer, Nathalia Wright, describes as the "first work in marble other than a portrait to be executed by one American at the order of another." That work, known as *The Chanting Cherubs*, created a sensation, amid mixed reviews, when it was exhibited in Boston and New York. It was also Cooper who introduced Greenough to Lafayette in Paris in the fall of 1831, in the hope of persuading the great man to sit for a portrait. Lafayette agreed with the stipulation that Cooper be present at all the sittings. Morse, who had already renewed his friendship with Greenough in Florence, joined him and Cooper in Paris. The three became inseparable companions, drawn together by their desire to discover "the means of renovating art." Although Greenough came to Washington in 1842 to oversee the installation of his statue of Washington in the Capitol, he did not return to the United States to take up residence until 1851. He died unexpectedly the following year in Somerville, Massachusetts.

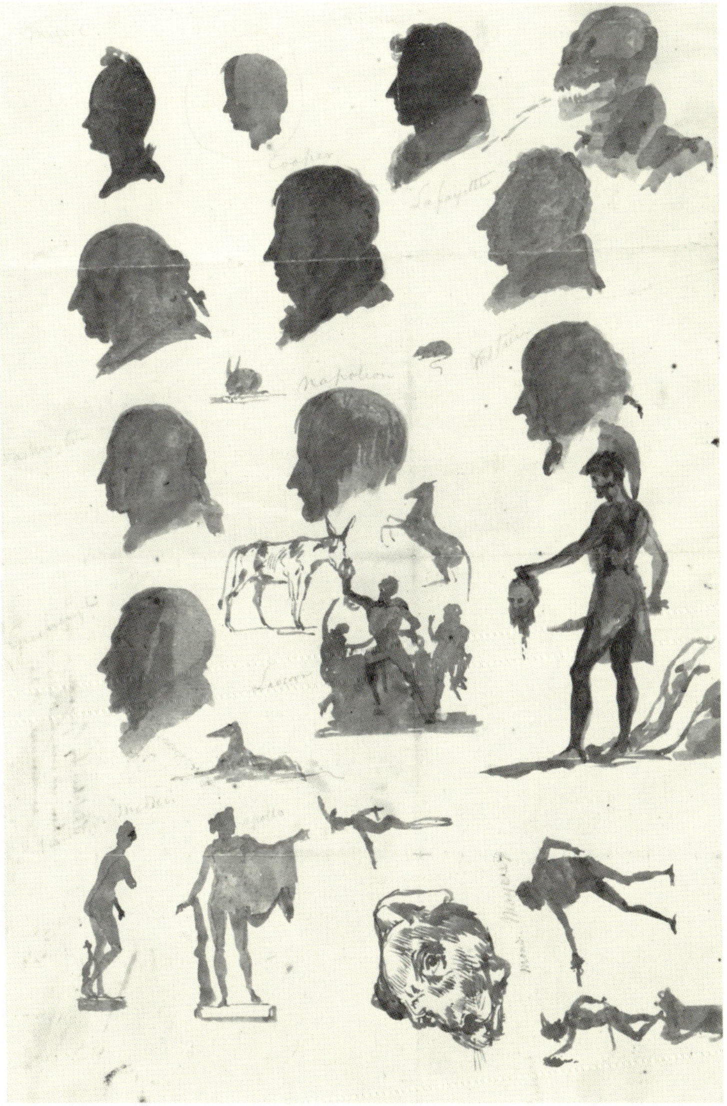

NO. 12 CHARLES WEBSTER HAWTHORNE (1872-1930)

Elderly woman in a Cap, 1907
Pencil on cream paper; 15 x 11 in.

Exh: The Paintings of Charles Hawthorne (Storrs, Connecticut, The University of Connecticut, 1968), no. 16, illus.; *American Portrait Drawings* (Washington, D.C., The National Portrait Gallery, 1980), pp. 108-109, illus.

Prov: Estate of artist, 1978; Marvin S. Sadik, Falmouth, Maine, until 1982.

Hawthorne was brought up in a small town near the coast of Maine. Little is known of his childhood and interest in art until he came to New York at eighteen to begin his studies at the Art Students League. In 1893 he attended Frank Vincent DuMond's evening classes and in the following two years also worked under George de Forest Brush and H. Siddons Mowbray. In the summer of 1896 he went to study at William M. Chase's school at Shinnecock, Long Island. Not long afterward Chase invited him to help organize his New York School and assist him at Shinnecock during the 1897 season. However, by 1898, Hawthorne decided to go to Holland to study, settling near Haarlem where he had access to the best work of Frans Hals. The bravura brushwork of the Dutch master was to have an enduring influence on his work. The year following his return home, he opened his own summer school at the fishing village of Provincetown, Massachusetts, which was destined to flourish for thirty years. Like Hals in some of his memorable pictures, Hawthorne became fascinated with the fishing folk of Provincetown and made them his subjects. In later years he went to Italy where he became particularly interested in the work of Renaissance masters like Tintoretto. During this period he painted a number of rapid watercolor landscape sketches of places he visited here and abroad, but Hawthorne was primarily at ease with oil and his teaching lays emphasis on painting as an artist's most personal statement—"a good painting is an excitement, an aesthetic emotion." With this in mind, it is not surprising to discover so few drawings. According to Marvin S. Sadik, the foremost Hawthorne scholar, this drawing is one of only five or six known works by the artist in the medium.

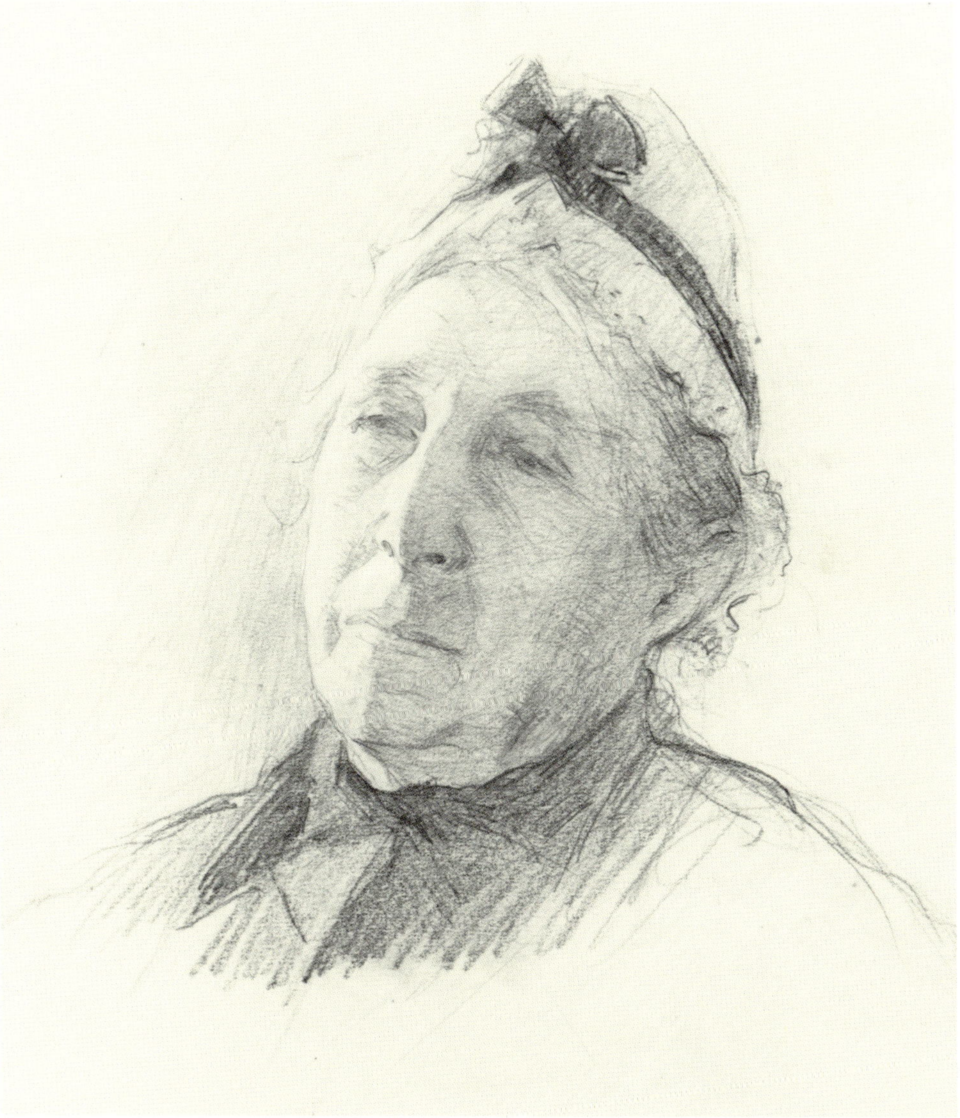

NO. 13 ROBERT HENRI (1865-1929)

Laughing Child, 1907
Charcoal; $9\,^1/_2$ x $7\,^5/_8$ in.

Inscribed, verso: "Robert Henri drew this head on the margin of my paper to show me a point he wished to put over in his New York art class in 1907/ Sketchingly Jack Sears." (According to Bennard B. Perlman, in a letter of August 30, 1982, "Jack Sears must have studied with Henri at the New York School of Art, the former Chase School, in 1907 since that is the only institution in which he taught that year.")

Prov: Jack Sears (1865-1969), Salt Lake City, Utah; Joyce Treiman, Los Angeles, California, until 1974.

Henri was born in Cincinnati, and began his studies in art in Philadelphia at the Pennsylvania Academy under Thomas P. Anshutz and Thomas Hovenden. He went to Paris in 1888 for a year to continue his formal studies at the Academy Julian and the Ecole des Beaux Arts, afterward traveling to Spain and Italy. He returned to Philadelphia in 1891 to teach at the Woman's School of Design, but left to return to Paris in 1894 for a longer stay. Back in the United States in 1897, he settled in New York and soon afterward began what was to be a thirty-year career as a teacher which was interrupted only by further trips to Spain, Holland, and Ireland, as well as in this country. Henri's connection with the future "Eight" group of artists actually began in Philadelphia in 1892 when he became acquainted with William Glackens and John Sloan. The three established the short-lived Charcoal Club in 1893, and Henri afterward started a discussion group in his studio which was attended regularly by Sloan and Glackens, and later joined by George Luks and Everett Shinn. He was the only member of the Philadelphia group without experience as a newspaper illustrator, but his paintings and drawings show that he was equally observant of life about him. He influenced and guided his artist friends and, through his inspired teaching, tried to emancipate the art spirit of the country. The one-time show of "The Eight" at Macbeth Gallery in 1908, which also included Arthur B. Davies, Maurice Prendergast, and Ernest Lawson, was a gesture that was intended as much to redirect American taste as it was to encourage other artists to free their self-expression. This spontaneous and expressive drawing, which can be dated just prior to the historic show of "The Eight," is also closely related to Henri's painting of the same subject which was included in the exhibition (coll. Whitney Museum of American Art).

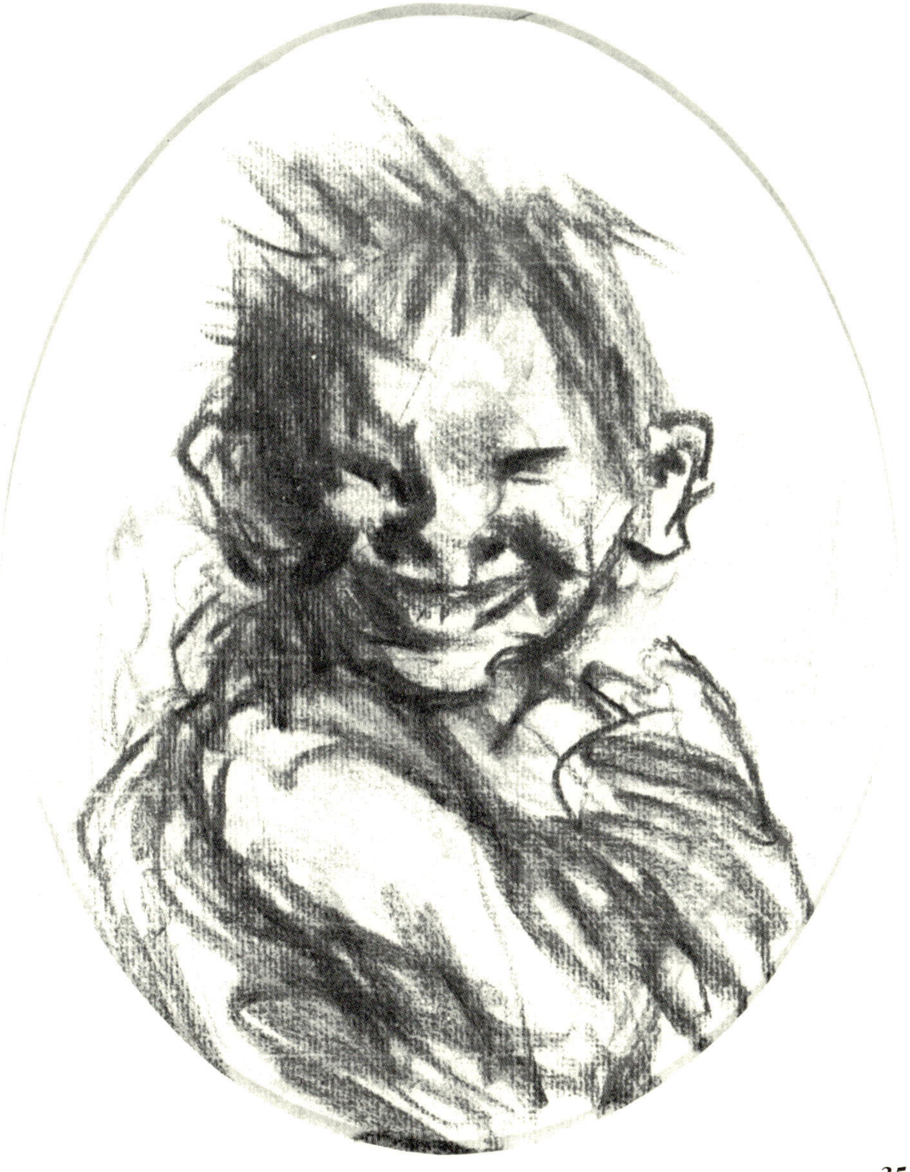

NO. 14 WINSLOW HOMER (1836-1910)

The Ballet at Niblo's Garden, 1859/1860

Pencil and gray wash, heightened with white, on tan paper; 5³/₈ x 8⁷/₈ in.

Signed, lower left:WH

Prov: The artist; presented to Alfred Cornelius Howland (1838-1909); descended in Howland family until 1975; Terry De Lapp, Los Angeles, California.

A double-sided drawing with thumbnail sketches on the verso of various figures and a classical head.

When Homer arrived in New York in the fall of 1859, he took lodgings at a boarding-house on East Sixteenth Street. Among his fellow-boarders were Alfred C. Howland, an aspiring young painter, and his brother Henry, later Judge Howland, who became his close friends. At the time Homer worked as a free-lance illustrator for *Harper's Weekly,* and his first published illustration of New York in 1859 was a double-page Christmas drawing showing various scenes of city life. The present drawing, apparently unpublished, most likely represents the Ravel ballet company that attracted a large audience in Boston before it opened at Niblo's Garden in New York on December 19, 1859 for a three-week run before leaving for performances in the south. The drawing is closely related in concept, subject matter, and compositional detail to Homer's previously published illustration in *Ballou's Pictorial,* Boston, March 12, 1859, titled "La Petite Angelina and Miss C. Thompson at the Boston Museum."

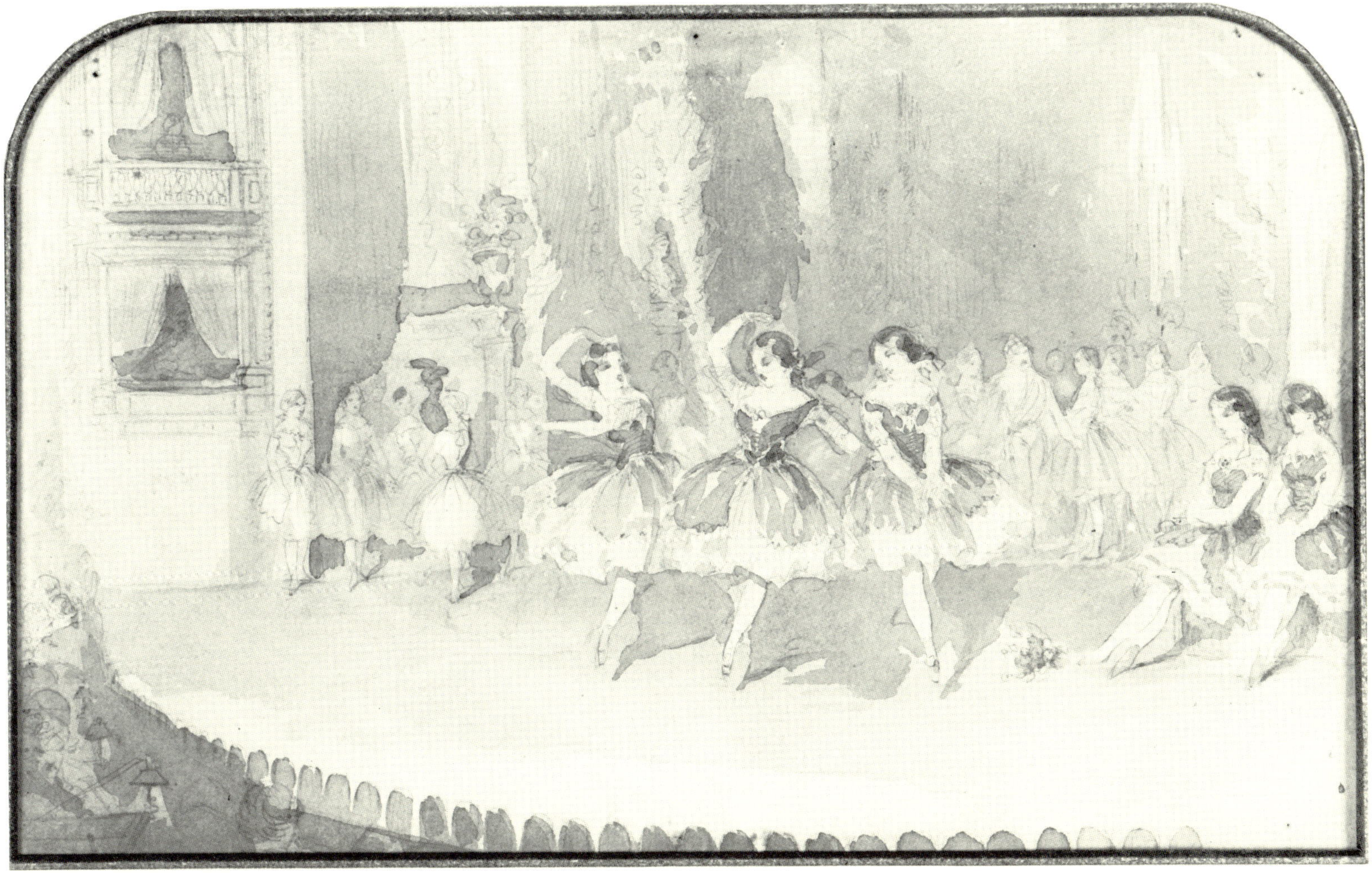

No. 15 Thomas Hovenden (1840-1895)

A Woman in Costume, 1878
Pencil, heightened with white, on gray paper; 12 x 7 3/8 in.

Signed and dated, lower right: T. Hovenden/1878/Paris

Hovenden went to Paris in 1874 to further his studies in painting. He first attended art schools in his native Ireland and in London before coming to the United States in 1863. In New York he entered the art school of the National Academy and, in 1867, the Academy exhibited his work for the first time. During the several years he spent abroad after 1874 he exhibited at the Paris Salons and joined a number of his fellow artists in founding an art colony at Pont Aven. Since Hovenden also continued to exhibit regularly at home, he returned to New York in 1880 with an already established reputation. By the time he joined the faculty of the Pennsylvania Academy of the Fine Arts in 1886, he was one of the most highly regarded painters in fashionable academic circles, famous for his subjects of contemporary life that combined descriptive realism with moral sentiment. Robert Henri was among his students during the first two years of his teaching at the Academy. His career was cut short in a train accident.

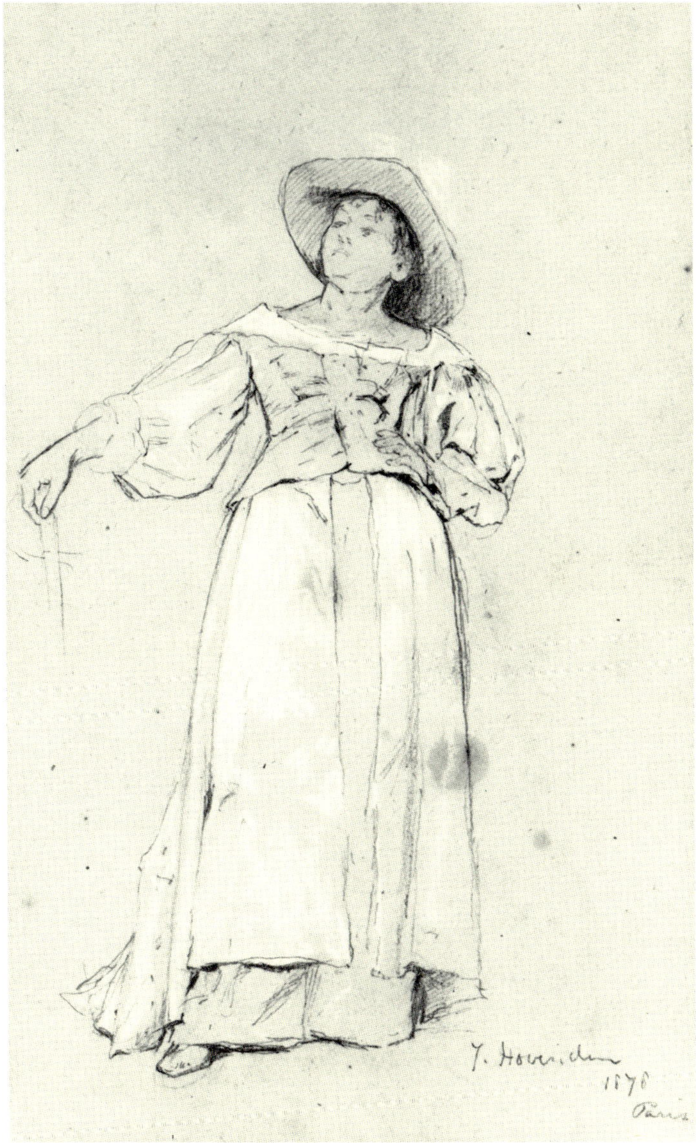
T. Hovenden
1878
Paris

No. 16 William Morris Hunt (1824-1870)

The Sick Donkey, 1868
Charcoal on buff paper; $11^{1}/_{2}$ x $17^{1}/_{2}$ in.

Signed and dated lower right: WMH.68

Exh: Exhibition of the Works of William Morris Hunt (Boston, Massachusetts, Museum of Fine Arts, 1879), no. 215: "Original Sketch of 'The Sick Donkey' "

Lit: American Art Review, I, 1880, pp. 98, 99, illus.

Prov: The Hon. Dwight Foster, Boston,Massachusetts; Auction, Christie's, New York, Sept. 26, 1986, lot 6.

Hunt was born in Brattleboro, Vermont, the son of a member of Congress, who died when he was eight. At the time the family moved to New Haven, Connecticut, where he received his first lessons in art from a local artist. Sent to Harvard for an academic education, he left in his senior year when his mother decided to take the family to Europe. Arriving in Rome in 1843 he studied sculpture with Henry Kirke Brown for a year before transferring to Düsseldorf to continue his studies at the Academy. By 1846 he decided to move to Paris in order to enter the atelier of Couture, the leading academic painter of the day. At the same time, his younger brother, Richard Morris Hunt, enrolled in the Ecole des Beaux Arts to study architecture under Lefuel, the first American to be trained there. By going to Paris, both young men were unknowingly breaking new ground in the direction American artists were soon to take in the choice of study abroad. In the five years Hunt worked with Couture, he learned to appreciate the spontaneous effects he could attain in the use of charcoal for drawing and application of oil for painting in a similar way. By 1852 he had also seen the work of Jean-François Millet at the Paris Salon. He met the painter and soon began to make the frequent visits to Barbizon that culminated in his moving there. Hunt remained in Barbizon for two years, becoming a close friend and disciple of Millet. When he returned to the United States in 1855 he married and began a professional career in Newport which also included teaching. Having moderate success he took a studio in Boston and, in 1867, took his family on an extended tour of Europe that included Paris, England, Belgium, Holland, and Italy. Back in Boston again, he devoted much of his time to teaching, with considerable success. Following a devastating studio fire in 1872, in which much of his work and personal collection of Barbizon pictures was destroyed, Hunt traveled as far as Florida and Mexico. But when he received the commission to paint two murals for the State Capitol at Albany, New York, in 1878, he was actively painting at a new studio he built in Magnolia, Massachusetts. The Albany mural commission was not only destined to be his last and most ambitious project, but also the most important work of its kind yet awarded to an American painter in this country. Frederic P. Vinton, who wrote the memorial article on Hunt for the *American Art Review* in 1880, passed up the artist's more typical landscape and still-life charcoal sketches in favor of "The Sick Donkey," which he reproduced in heliotype to emphasize its use of material and texture. He also felt that the drawing had "an added interest, as it shows the artist as a composer." In adopting a classically structured composition of figures in an architectural setting to express the individual character of a simple motive, Hunt demonstrated in this significant drawing the substance of what he had absorbed from the years of study and observation he spent with Couture and Millet.

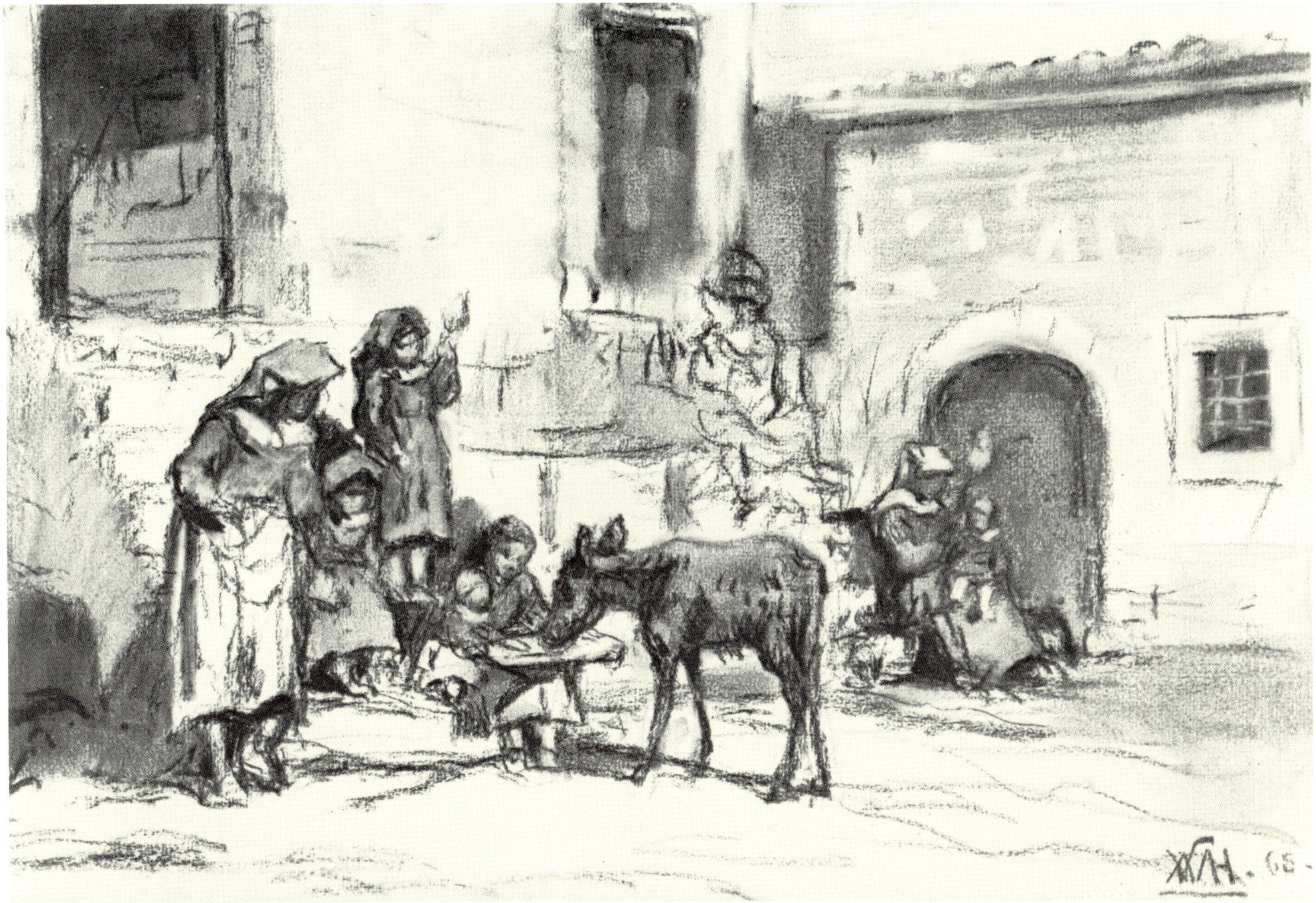

No. 17 Daniel Huntington (1816-1906)

Portrait of Charles Lanman, ca. 1840
Pencil; 7 x 5 1/2 in.

Signed, lower right: DH. del.

Prov: Charles Lanman, Georgetown, D.C.

Huntington and the subject, Lanman, were close contemporaries who shared a lifetime friendship and professional association. This sensitive portrait drawing documents their relationship during Lanman's early years in New York where he worked as a clerk, writer, and artist. He became an Associate Member of the National Academy of Design in 1842. Lanman's essay on "Our New York Painters," which was published in 1845 in his *Letters from a Landscape Painter*, describes Huntington as having "provided many admirable pictures, which place him on a level with the most gifted artists of any country." In his unpublished reminiscences, written about 1889, he describes his continuing admiration for the artist in even warmer terms: "My love for the man and my very high regard for the artist has never known a moment's abatement; and I only regret that I cannot indite a laudatory poem in his honor instead of this tame and prosy record of my recollections. . . . During my residence in New York from 1835 to 1847, there was hardly a place in the city which I occasionally visited with more pleasure than the studio of Daniel Huntington."

Huntington displayed some talent for drawing during the year he spent at Yale. In 1832 he transferred to Hamilton College and there met Charles Loring Elliott who took him on as one of his pupils. That brief experience evidently encouraged him to consider a career in painting. After he left college in 1835, he went to New York to study under Samuel F. B. Morse, then President of the National Academy, and with Henry Inman. He went abroad for the first time in 1839, traveling to Rome, Florence, and Paris. Huntington was to make further trips to Europe in the early 1840s and 1850s, and as late as 1882. A prolific landscape, history, and portrait painter, he enjoyed a distinguished career in New York, where he was elected a full Member of the National Academy in 1840, and served as its President from 1862-1870, and again from 1877-1890. By far the most comprehensive collection of his drawings is in the Cooper-Hewitt Museum in New York.

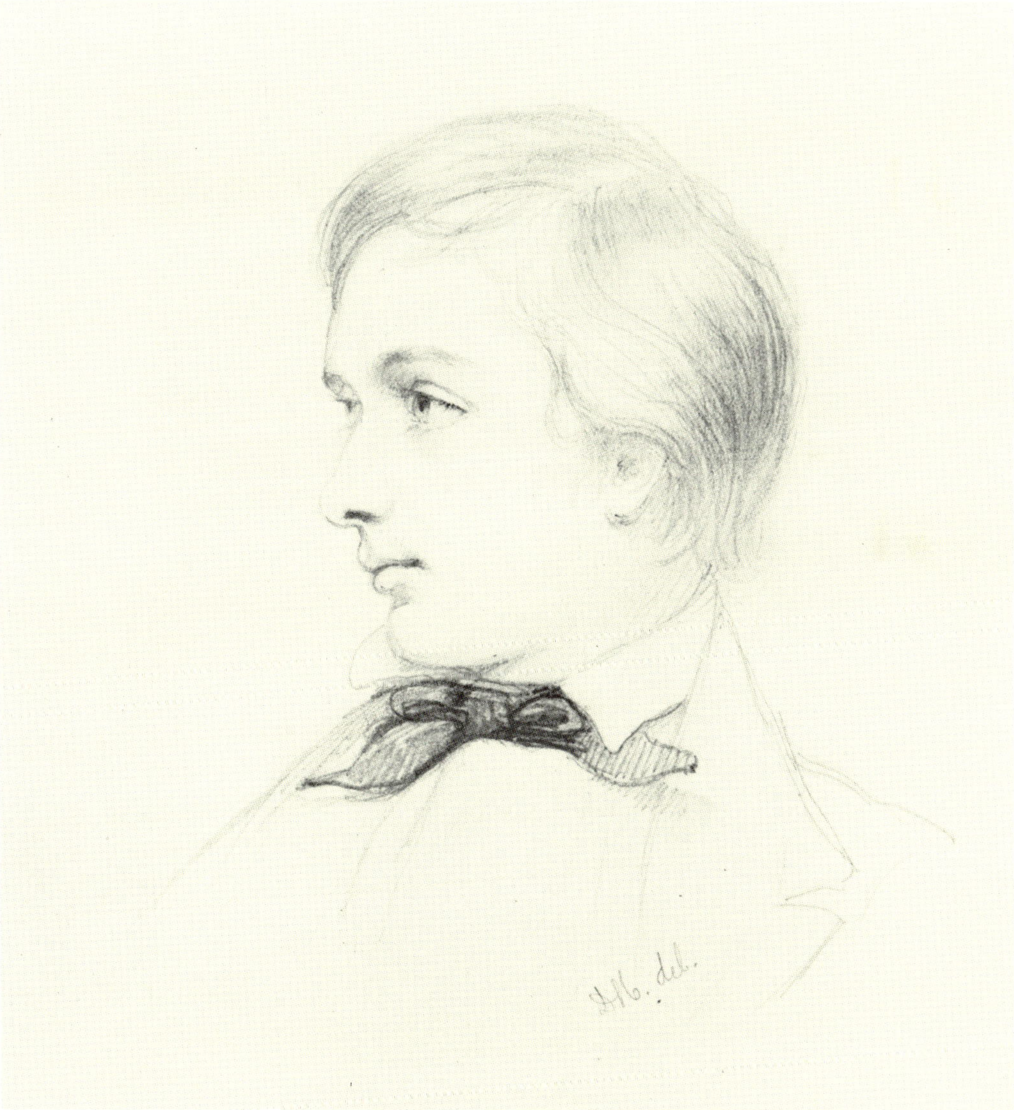

NO. 18 JOHN WESLEY JARVIS (1780-1840)

Portrait of Jacob Housman, ca. 1809
Gray wash; 4 1/2 x 3 1/2 in.(sight)

Prov: A.J. Boggs; Marvin S. Sadik, Falmouth, Maine. A portrait of Housman, a New York merchant, was painted by Jarvis in 1809 (coll. Detroit Institute of Arts). This drawing, said to be of the same subject, dates from about the same period.

Jarvis was born in England, the son of an American father and an English mother. He was brought to America when he was about five, the family ultimately settling in Philadelphia. Young Jarvis evidently received encouragement in art early, largely through artist friends like Matthew Pratt and Jeremiah Paul, but he learned the fundamentals of painting and engraving from Edward Savage, to whom he was apprenticed from about 1796 to 1801. He was on his own by 1802 when he opened an engraving workshop in New York, but by the following year he entered into a partnership with the miniaturist Joseph Wood. They advertised themselves as portrait and miniature painters, drawing instructors, engravers, and print-sellers. It also seems evident that physionotrace portraits brought in the most business. Jarvis' reputation as a wit, story-teller, tippler, and pleasure-seeker began with his relationship with his equally lively partner. The partnership ended in 1810 when Jarvis decided on portrait-painting as a career. With studios in New York, he became known for his facility to capture accurate likeness and soon enjoyed a distinguished patronage. He also traveled south to Baltimore, Richmond, Charleston, and New Orleans to take on portrait commissions. He exhibited regularly at the American Academy and the Pennsylvania Academy, and occasionally at the newly-formed National Academy. His declining fortunes, accompanied by deteriorating health, apparently began about 1830, and he was compelled to cease all artistic activity by 1834. Although Jarvis was not a first-rate painter, he was at his best in his sketches and miniature portrait drawings in which he often captured lively expression and character with obvious facility.

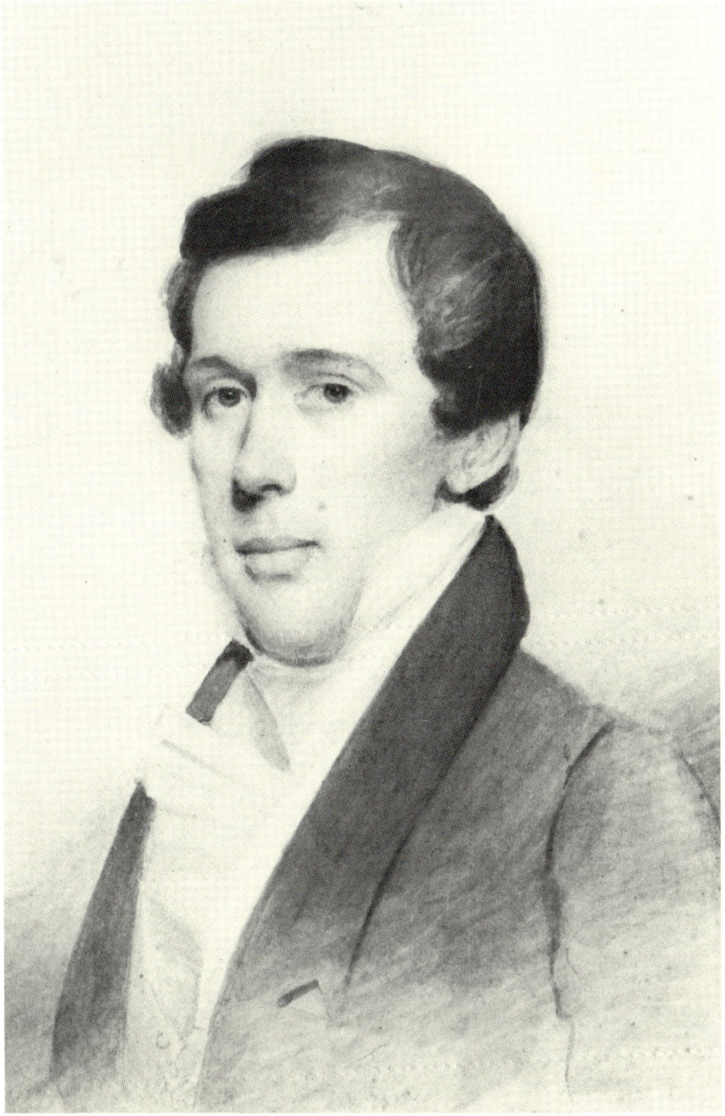

No. 19 [Jonathan] Eastman Johnson
(1824-1906)

Reclining Man, 1849/1851

Pencil on brown paper; 8 1/4 x 11 in.

Exh: Eastman Johnson, an American Genre Painter (Brooklyn, New York, The Brooklyn Museum, 1940), no. 454, Pl. XL.

Prov: The artist; descended in family to granddaughter, Baroness Muriel van Reigersberg Versluys, Paris (1940); Hirschl & Adler Galleries, New York.

Born in Lowell, Massachusetts, Johnson displayed a special gift for drawing early in life; but his career had its beginnings in Boston when, at sixteen, he began working for the commercial lithographer, John H. Bufford. He was on his own a year later traveling along the east coast making crayon portraits at modest prices. He left America in 1849 to enroll at the Düsseldorf Academy for a course of formal study that was noted for its emphasis on precise drawing and anatomy rather than painting. Somewhat disenchanted after two years, Johnson left to go to Holland to study the works of Rembrandt, Hals, and Dutch genre painters of same period, making The Hague his headquarters. He returned home in 1855 leaving behind a considerable reputation he had made in the Dutch city as a portrait painter. For the next four years he traveled about the country before settling in New York in 1859. By 1860 he was a full Member of the National Academy, where he had been exhibiting regularly since 1855, and was to continue to do so until the end of his life. The pictures he exhibited included portraits, crayon drawings, as well as the narrative paintings which have given him enduring fame. Although New York was his permanent residence, Johnson spent the summers in Nantucket, Massachusetts, and he also traveled abroad in his later years. This drawing reflects the thorough grounding in draftsmanship Johnson received during the two years of study he spent at the Düsseldorf Academy. The emphasis on line over tone suggests a probable dating within the Düsseldorf years rather than the succeeding period in Holland in which chiaroscuro effects were the dominant features he quickly absorbed from his study of the Dutch masters.

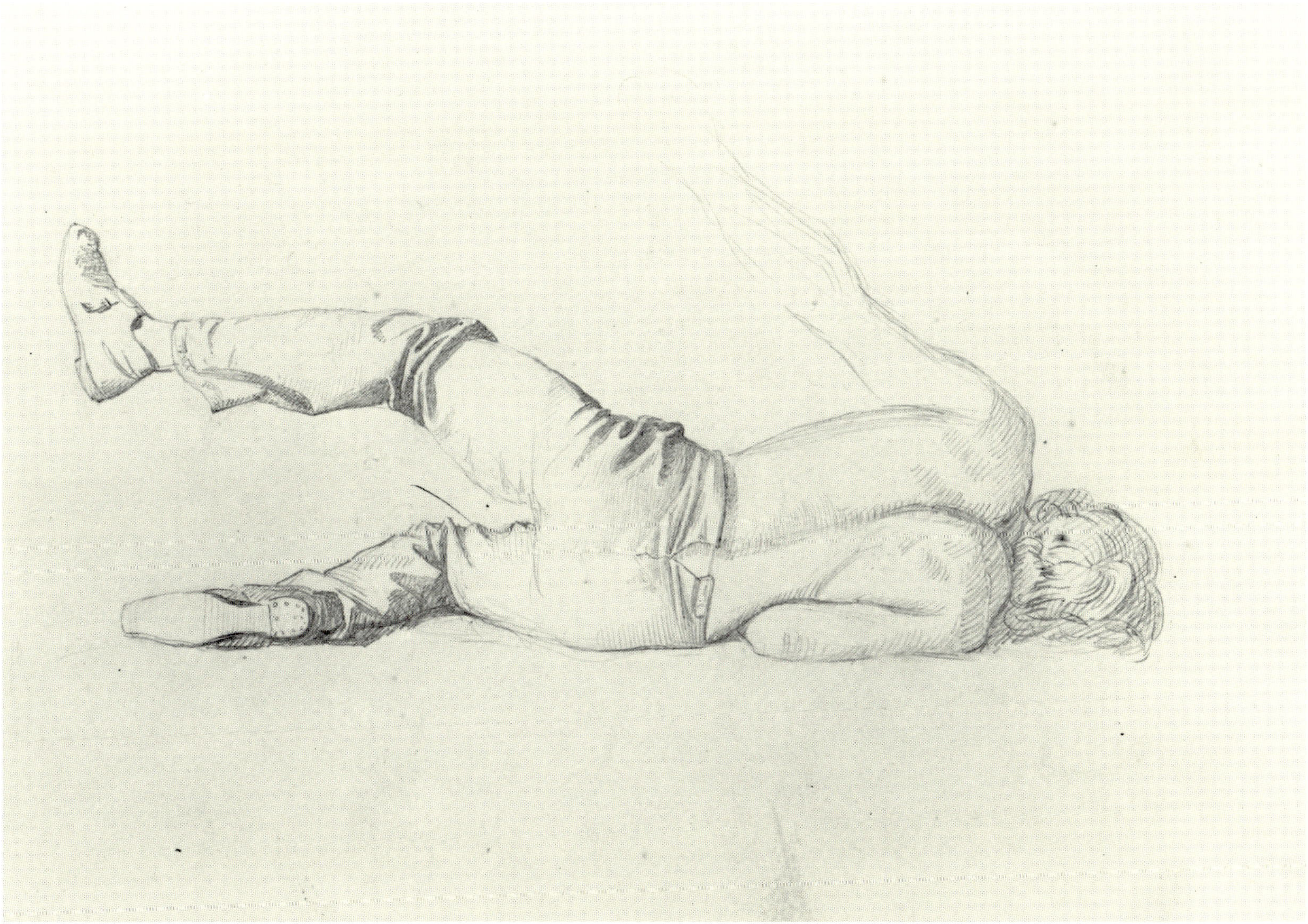

NO. 20 JOHN LA FARGE (1835-1910)

The Angel Stirring the Pool: Study for the Dr. James Ayer Memorial Window, Mount Vernon Church, Boston, 1896/1898

Watercolor over pencil; Two panels: 17 1/4 x 7 3/4 in., (left lancet); 17 5/8 x 8 1/8 in., (right lancet).

Left panel signed and dated in ink, lower left: JLF-1896; right panel signed and dated in ink, lower right: JLF.98. Inscribed in margin, lower right: Copyrighted, John La Farge 1898/Angel Troubling the Waters of the Pool of Bethesda.

Exh: Architectural League, New York, 1899, no. 36 ("Colored Sketch for the Ayer Memorial Window, Mount Vernon Church, Boston"); John La Farge one-man show, Montross Gallery, New York, 1901, no. 22 ("The Angel Stirring the Pool").

Lit: Russell Sturgis, "A Pictorial Window," New York *Evening Post*, November 7, 1898, p. 4; H. Barbara Weinberg, *The Decorative Work of John La Farge* (New York and London, Garland Publishing Co., 1977), pp. 423-425. Henry La Farge, James L. Yarnell, and Mary A. La Farge, *The Catalogue Raisonné of the Works of John La Farge*, Vol. 1, forthcoming from Yale University Press.

Prov: Estate of the artist; George Breed Zug, Chicago and Hanover, New Hampshire, 1911-after 1927; James W. Barney, New York (d. 1946); Parke-Bernet Galleries, New York, auction, Sept. 18-21, 1946, no. 558 (Barney estate); A. Loewy, New York, 1946; Kennedy Galleries, New York, by 1960.

The window was commissioned of La Farge in 1896 by Dr. James B. Ayer of Boston in memory of his father, Dr. James Ayer (1815-1891). It was designed for the nave, east wall, of Mount Vernon Church, Boston, and dedicated in November, 1898.

La Farge was born in New York, of French parentage. His father, a prosperous businessman, provided him with the cultured surroundings and college education that were to have a lasting impact on his life. In 1856, a year of European travel refined his cultural awareness and deepened his interest in art. La Farge's decision to study art under William Morris Hunt was, in 1859, rather more an intellectual process than a need for technical direction, but it was to be a decisive experience. Shortly afterward, he began to paint seriously. The early works were landscapes and small still-lifes of intimate objects that were mainly experiments in the phenomena of light and color, anticipating Impressionism in America by some years. His work from the outset also reflected a penetrating observation of nature and a use of pure color that bonded the precepts of the Barbizon men with the English Pre-Raphaelites, artists he had particularly admired during his year abroad. In the 1860s he began to make a name for himself with illustrations for *Riverside Magazine*, and for books like Tennyson's *Enoch Arden* (1868).

La Farge's involvement with the creative possibilities of painting in an architectural environment made him the only American artist qualified to take on the important

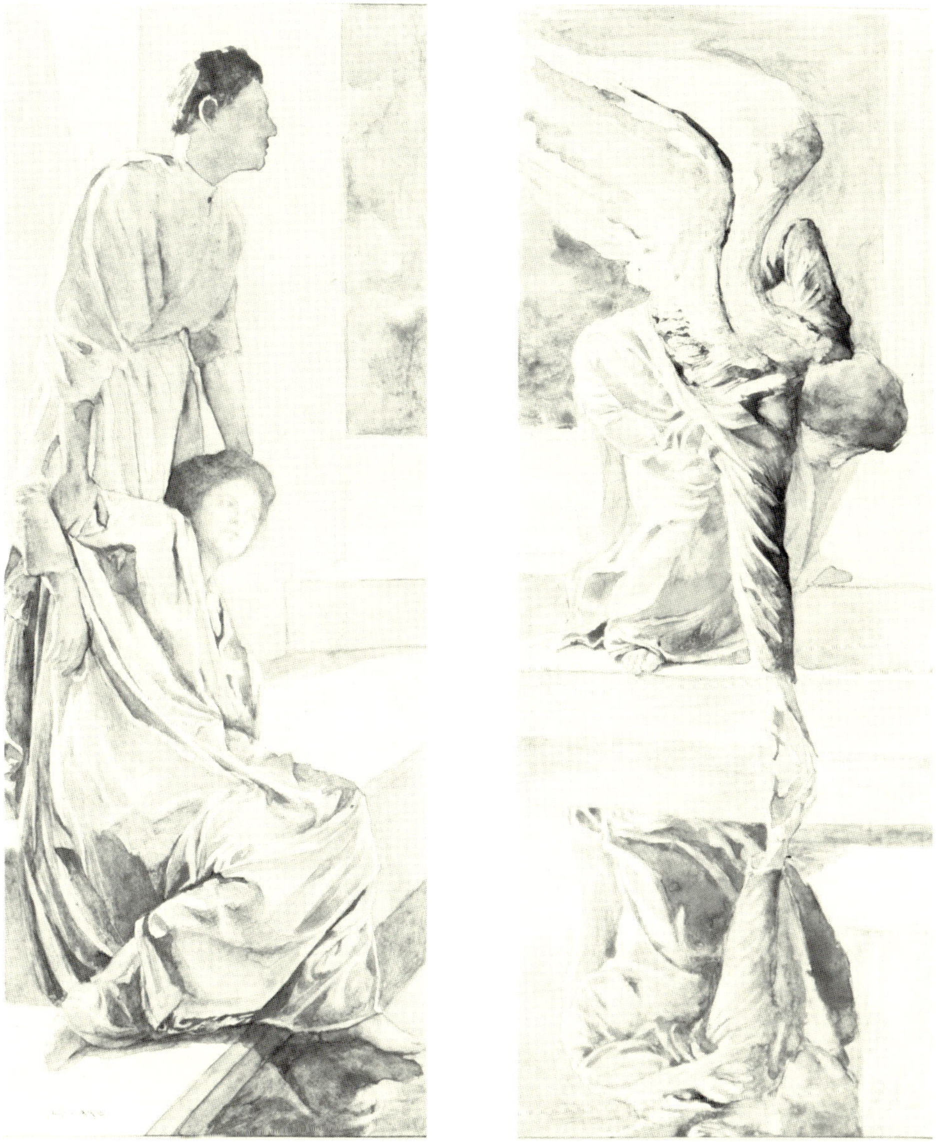

JOHN LA FARGE
(Continued)

decorative projects that came his way within the next few years. In 1877, H.H. Richardson invited him to assume the direction of the mural decorations for Trinity Church in Boston. The glowing success of that project brought him numerous other prestigious commissions, including St. Thomas' and the Church of the Ascension in New York, and the State Capitol of Minnesota. At about the same time, his preoccupation with problems of light and color was transferred to the designing and production of glass windows, the only artist in the 1870s to experiment in that medium. The idea of using opalescent glass to replace traditional stained glass represented an inventive spirit that was to be unrivaled until Louis C. Tiffany appeared on the scene in the 1880s. Both men were ultimately credited with having invented and perfected a new style and technique in glass. Most of his energy in his middle years was devoted to mural decoration, as well as to filling orders for the design and manufacture of windows across the country. His continued passion for color was revitalized by a trip to Japan and the South Seas with his close friend Henry Adams in 1886. In his later years he lectured and wrote several books on his travels and on painting. Royal Cortissoz afterward stated that "a lot of brain stuff went into his work, regardless of subject," considering La Farge "a great artist who was a great soul," (New York, The Metropolitan Museum of Art, *An Exhibition of the Work of John La Farge*, March 23 to April 26, 1936, pp. 7, 16).

Although La Farge often used charcoal for his drawings, the color possibilities of watercolor made it the medium he was to use most consistently throughout his career. This watercolor is the only recorded color study for the Ayer Memorial window, the two other studies (unlocated) being working drawings in pencil. Since Ayer was a medical man by profession, the subject selected was taken from the New Testament, John 5:2-4, relating to the miraculous healing of the sick, blind, and lame at the Pool of Bethesda by the angel of the Lord. The interpretation of the subject in glass provided La Farge's adventuresome spirit with a new challenge. Russell Sturgis reported that the artist constructed a pool on his studio to study reflections and to effect an illusion which Sturgis believed had not yet been attempted in glass.

NO. 21 WILL HICOK LOW (1853-1932)

Gloria in Excelsis Deo in Terra Paix, 1884
Pencil, heightened with white, on Bristol board; 13 1/2 x 10 7/8 in.

Signed, dated, and inscribed, lower left: à l'ami Faxon/ Dec 1884 Will H. Low.

Prov: The artist; presented to William Bailey Faxon; Mrs. Gabriel Engel, New York.

Low had no previous directed study in art before he went to France in 1873. He was chiefly self-taught throughout his youth in Albany, and later in New York. Nonetheless he was able to gain employment as a free-lance illustrator for *Harper's Weekly* at that time. Serious study came during the five years he spent in Paris in the ateliers of Gérome and Carolus-Duran. The traditional academic experience he received under Gérome in particular had a profound influence on the mature work he produced as an illustrator and mural painter on his return to the United States in 1878. Like Kenyon Cox, with whom he shared an almost identical training and experience, he represents the classical ideal in American art through the monumental murals he produced for public buildings, as well as through his lectures, teaching, and writing. Low also exhibited regularly at the National Academy for some twenty-five years, was elected an Associate of the Academy in 1888, and a full Member in 1890. Drawing was basic to Low all his professional life and he often quoted Ingres' maxim that "drawing is the probity of art." This highly finished presentation drawing combines the classical ideal with overtones of religious symbolism that owes much to Low's close observation of the Italian masters.

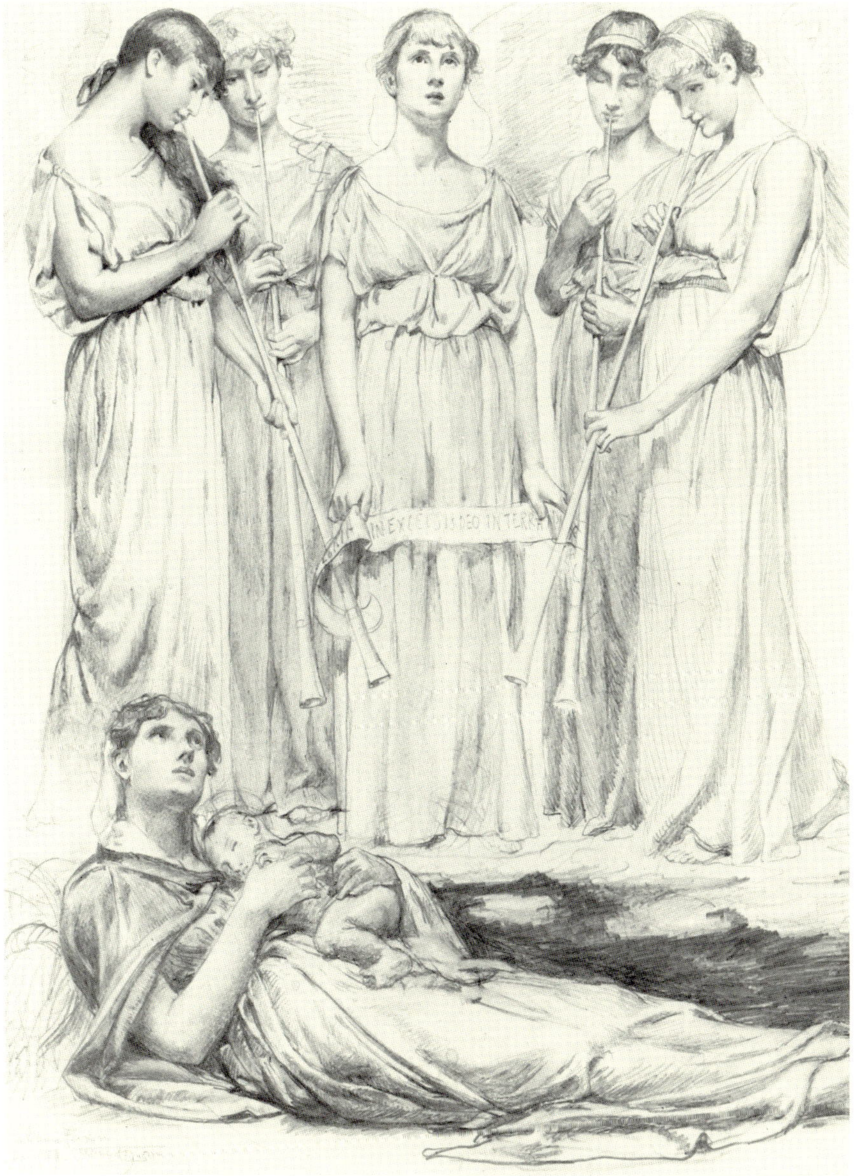

NO. 22 SAMUEL FINLEY BREESE MORSE (1791-1872)

Sketch of Contadini: Study for the "Chapel of the Virgin at Subiaco," 1830
Watercolor, pencil; 9 1/4 x 7 1/2 in.

Signed, dated, and inscribed, upper right: Sketch of Contadini/ made in Subiaco in the Sabine Hills/ 40 miles East of Rome Italy, by/ Samuel F. B. Morse in the year 1830/ Presented to John R. Chapin Esq./ from his friend/ Saml F. B. Morse/ Nov. 1856.

Exh: American Drawings and Watercolors, Hirschl & Adler Galleries, New York, October 6-29, 1979, no. 80; *American Art from the Colonial and Federal Periods*, Hirschl & Adler Galleries, New York, 1982, no. 71 (illus.); *Samuel F. B. Morse*, Grey Art Gallery, New York University, 1982, p. 67, fig. 70 (illus.), p. 89, no. 39.

Lit: The Quarterly Illustrator, III (9), January-March, 1895, p. 105 (illus.): John R. Chapin, "Random Recollections of a Veteran Illustrator."

Prov: The artist; presented to John R. Chapin, November, 1856; descended in Chapin family to Charles P. Chapin, grandson, until 1979; Hirschl & Adler Galleries, New York.

A working drawing for the painting commissioned by Stephen Salisbury of Worcester, Massachusetts, who was assured by Morse that it had been painted *con amore*. The painting was praised when it was exhibited at the Campidoglio in March, 1831. The painting actually exists in two versions, the first a sketch in oils, and the larger (Salisbury) version, now in the collection of the Worcester Art Museum.

In early May, 1830, Morse and other fellow-artists made a sketching trip to Tivoli, Subiaco, Vico, and Vara. He filled his notebooks with descriptions of the various places he visited. In his enthusiastic description of the place, it is obvious that the landscape, atmosphere, and people of Subiaco particularly appealed to him. It is reported that he returned to Rome on June 3 "after enjoying to the full this excursion, from which he brought back many sketches. . . ." Since so very few of Morse's preparatory sketches for his paintings have survived, this drawing is of the greatest significance in understanding his procedure. John R. Chapin, to whom Morse presented the drawing, was an illustrator and painter of battle scenes. He may have become acquainted with Morse during his art-student years in New York, possibly at the time Morse was a professor of drawing and painting at New York University.

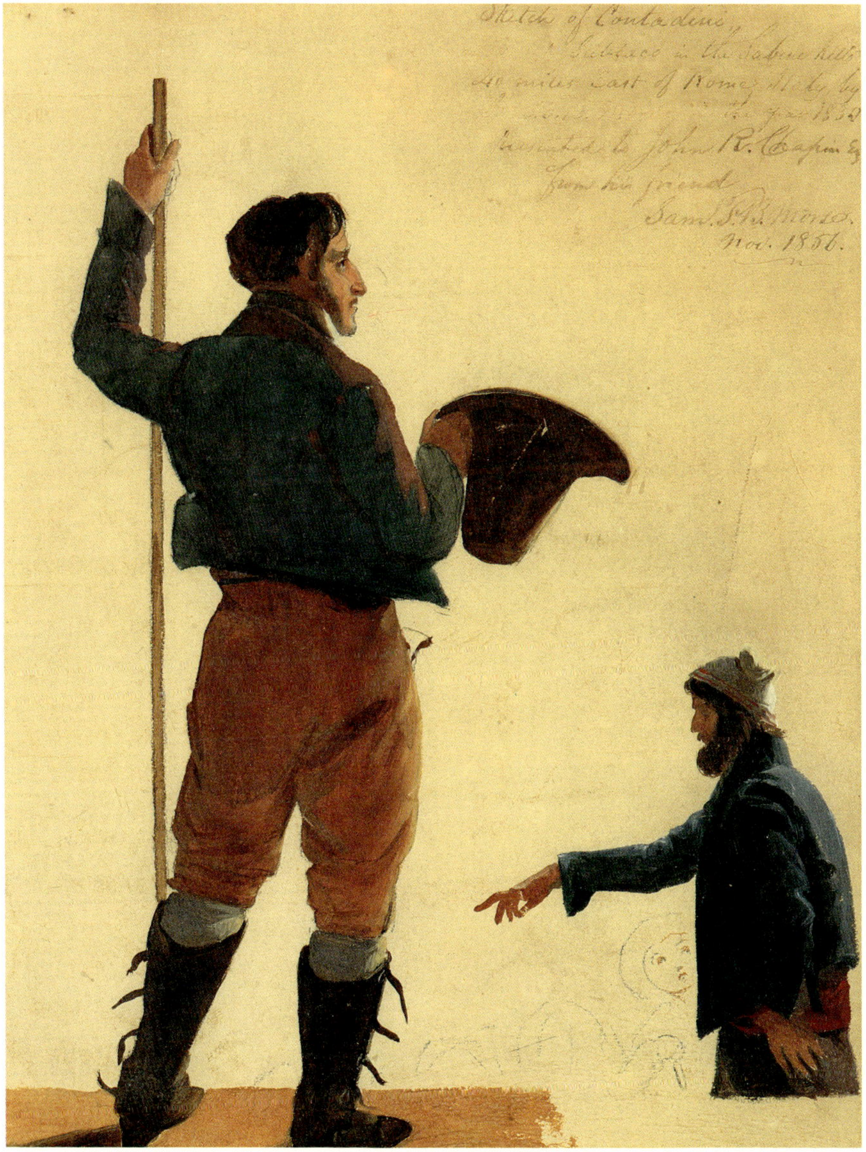
Sketch of Contadini,
40 miles East of Rome, Italy, by
presented to John R. Chapin Esq
from his friend
Saml. F.B. Morse.
Nov. 1856.

NO. 23 WILLIAM SIDNEY MOUNT (1807-1868)

Henry Smith Mount on his Deathbed, 1841
Pen and ink and watercolor; 7 1/2 x 7 3/4 in.

Signed and inscribed below: To Benjn F. Thompson Esqr./ A Sketch of Henry S. Mount who died the/ 10th of Jan. 1841, in the 39th year of his age./ taken after death by his brother Wm S. Mount. A later inscription by Benjamin Franklin Thompson, the recipient: See a brief notice of this amiable/ man, in my Hist. of Long Island vol./ 2. page 527 - 2 Edition -/ B.F. Thompson.

Lit: Alfred Frankenstein, *William Sidney Mount* (New York, Abrams [1975]), p. 62, fig. 22.

Prov: The artist; presented to Benjamin Franklin Thompson, 1841; Kennedy Galleries, New York.

William Sidney Mount was born at Setauket, Long Island, but grew up in nearby Stony Brook in a close family circle that encouraged his earliest artistic efforts. Two of his brothers, Henry and Shepard, were also ambitious to become painters from their boyhood years. Henry, the eldest, began his career in New York by learning to paint signboards. By 1824 he had established his own business, but yearned to become considerably more than a sign painter. Shepard was at first apprenticed to a carriage-maker, but reportedly spent all of his spare time learning how to paint portraits. William, the youngest, received special attention from Henry, who brought him to New York, ostensibly to learn the sign-painting trade, but more to support his efforts to gain entrance to the newly-formed art school of the National Academy. William was actually to remain about a year at the school, drawing chiefly from the antique, before returning to Stony Brook to work entirely on his own. By 1828 he began to exhibit regularly at the Academy and, in 1829, had moved back to New York to practice portrait painting, but it was a painting of Long Island country life he sent to the 1830 Academy show that earned his first recognition and determined his future course.

Mount was probably the first American-born painter to achieve a national reputation in his special field without the benefit of European study and, at least to some extent, because of it. He denied offers from two of his chief patrons, Luman Reed and Jonathan Sturges, to send him abroad and later rejected an invitation from his dealer, Goupil, who offered him a year in Paris. It is difficult to say whether this was a considered judgment on his part, but it seemed quite evident to contemporary critics that he had learned his craft well on his own, and an appreciative public had been quick to recognize his pictures as decidedly original and specifically American. One art critic, most likely Charles Lanman, discussed the important question in a newspaper article, published in 1847, which stated that the "grand tour" might, in fact, do "more injury than good," using Mount as living proof that he was "unquestionably without superior" in his "particular department," because he chose to remain at home, (New York *Evening Post*). The article displayed a "common sense" that was "greatly needed," (letter to Lanman, Stony Brook, New York, 9 March 1847, New-York Historical Society).

Never a prolific painter, Mount was, by comparison, an indefatigable draftsman who consistently made notations of pictorial ideas he filed away for future reference. Even after persistent illness compelled him to limit his painting even more, he continued to fill sketchbooks with drawings of genre subjects. The insistence on drawing from nature on expeditions he made on foot over the years ultimately led to the "Portable Studio" he devised and ordered constructed in 1861. This was a horse-drawn carriage, with plate glass walls on three sides and skylighted, which enabled him to continue such expeditions in greater comfort. Drawing was central to all of Mount's efforts, and he preserved every sketch with an eye to its possible use. He worked chiefly in pencil or pen-and-ink and less commonly, as in this

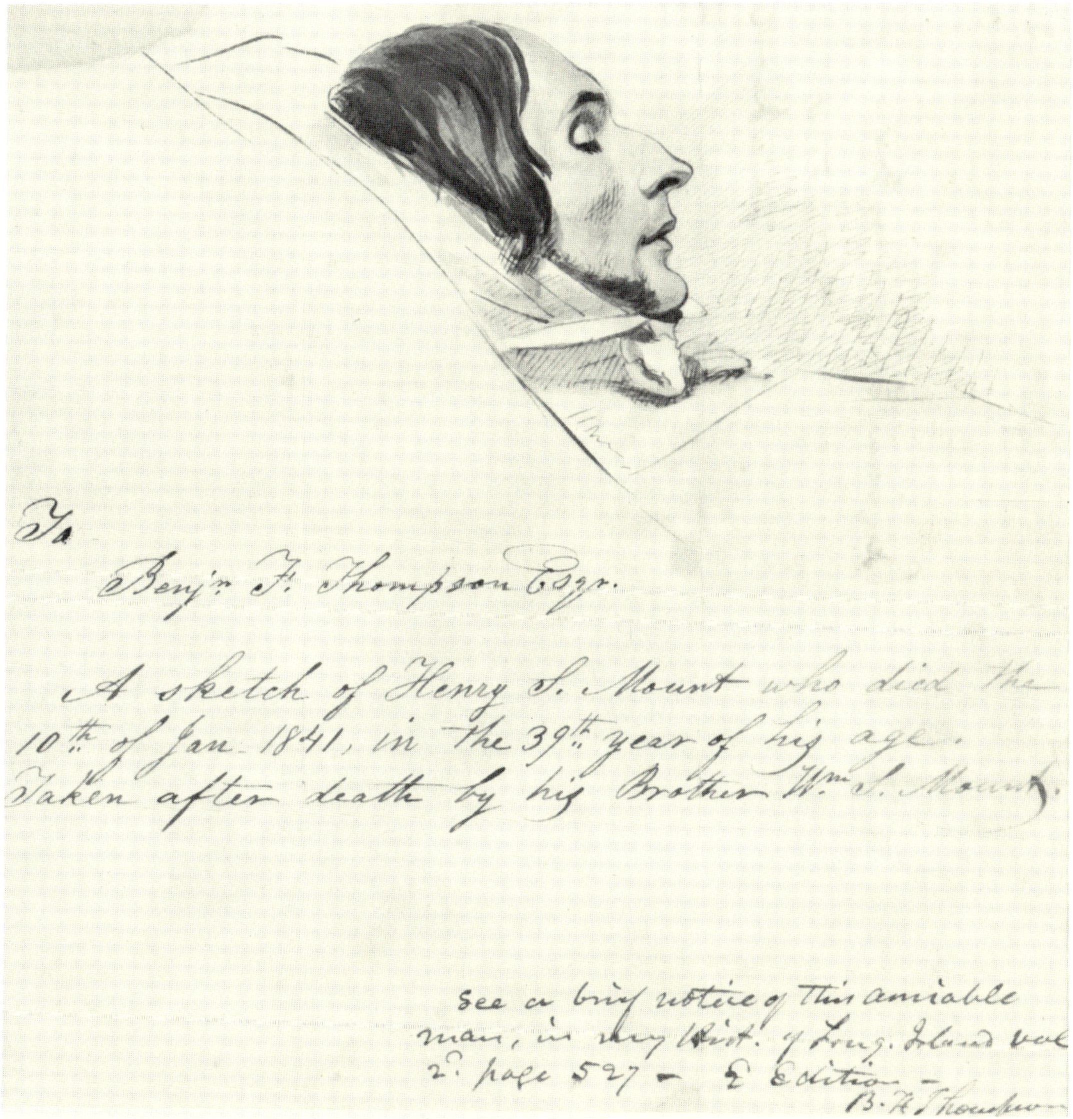

WILLIAM SIDNEY MOUNT
(Continued)

drawing of Henry, were they finished in watercolor. The finest examples of his craftsmanship are the portraits he made of friends and family. Drawings made after death, usually as preparatory studies for posthumous portrait commissions, occur regularly in Mount's work. It therefore must have seemed entirely appropriate for him to record his brother's features for family and friends, although apparently without a painting in mind. Mount made several sketches of Henry after his untimely death at Setauket in 1841, most of them replicas of the original and intended as memorial presentations to close family friends. The recipient in this instance, Benjamin Franklin Thompson (1784-1849), had been a friend and family confidant from the family's Setauket years. He encouraged the Mount brothers to consider making art a serious career. At first a physician, he later practiced law in Hempstead, and made a lasting reputation as the author of the *History of Long Island*, which was first published in 1839 and went through numerous subsequent editions.

NO. 24 JEROME MYERS (1867-1940)

Self-Portrait, ca. 1935
Sepia crayon on cream paper; 16 x 12 1/4 in.

Signed in pencil, lower right: Jerome Myers/ E.M. (signature added by Mrs. Jerome Myers (Ethel Myers).

Prov: The artist's estate; Mrs. Jerome Myers until 1958.

In his autobiography, *Artist in Manhattan* (American Artists Group, 1940), Myers discusses the deeper significance of the self-portrait: "In the mirror the artist comes face to face with himself in the many moods that life impresses on him. It may be in self-revelation, or a gay defiance to laugh with life or at it, to seize the fleeting moment of joy, to capture the symbol of happiness. Or perhaps to let the brush portray the care and thoughtfulness that the observant eye sees in the mirror's record of the changes Time has wrought . . . " (p. 117).

This drawing is one of the many self-portraits Jerome Myers produced in various media during his lifetime and he readily admitted his obvious kinship to Rembrandt in this respect. He was also proud of his own Dutch ancestry and felt that "Rembrandt's Dutch courage has sustained me, even as his art has inspired me. On faith and as an atavistic liberty, I have adopted him as an exemplar . . ." (p. 75).

Myers was born in Petersburg, Virginia, but spent his childhood in Trenton, New Jersey, Philadelphia, and Baltimore before the family settled in New York in 1886. At that time he earned a livelihood as a theater scene painter to support his art studies at the Cooper Union and the Art Students League. He was briefly in Paris in 1896 before returning permanently to New York where he soon began to paint the first of his pictures of life on Manhattan's East Side. In 1911 Myers joined with other artists to form the Association of American Painters and Sculptors which organized the momentous Armory Show that opened in New York in February 1913. Two paintings and fifteen drawings by Myers were included in the exhibition.

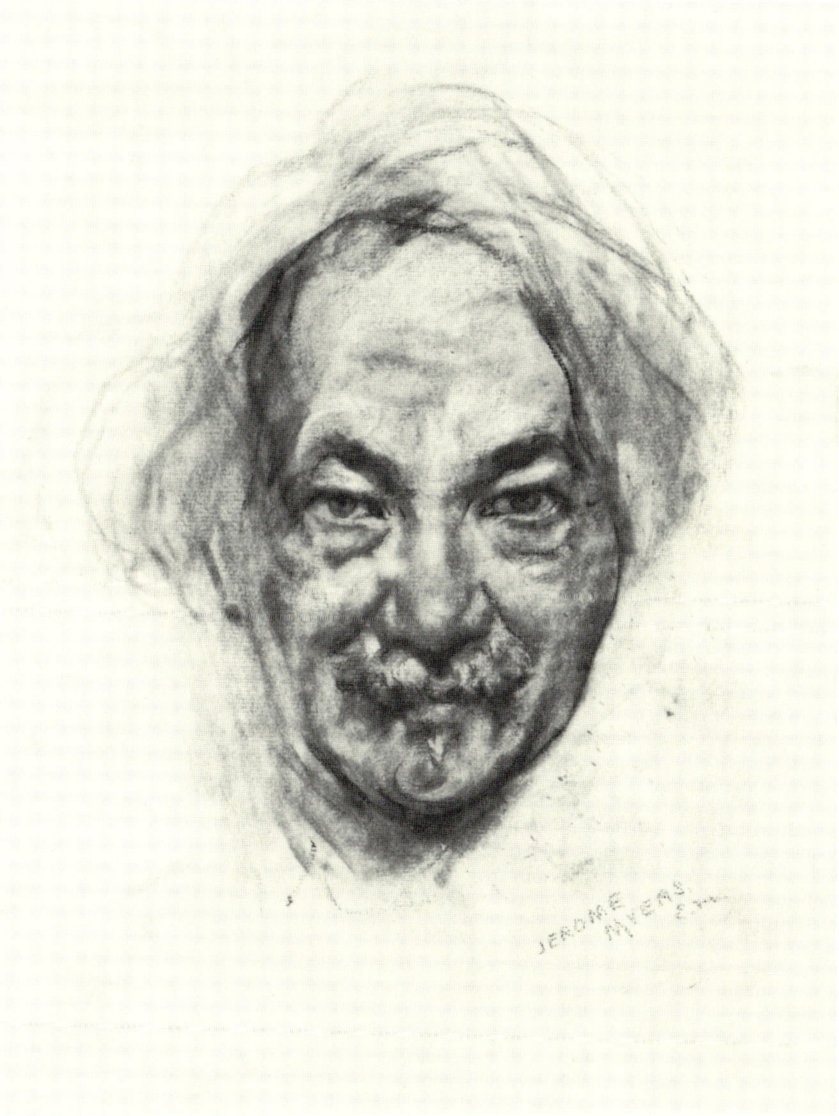
JEROME MYERS

NO. 25 HUGH NEWELL (1830-1915)

Impressionist, ca. 1878
Charcoal, heightened with white,on gray paper; 19 x 12 1/2 in.

Inscribed, lower right: Impressionist

Prov: The artist; descended in artist's family until 1966; Terry De Lapp, Los Angeles, California.

Newell was born in Ireland, studied art on the continent, first at the Académie d'Anvers and with Couture, before completing his studies at the Royal Academy in London. He came to America in 1851, beginning his professional career in Baltimore where he worked until 1860, afterward moving to Pittsburgh for several years. He apparently returned to Baltimore about 1879 and remained there until 1892. Working primarily in charcoal and pencil during his first Baltimore and Pittsburgh years, Newell's drawings are clearly still in the line of Winslow Homer and Eastman Johnson in both technique and in his preference for rural subjects. In the second Baltimore period his style moved closer to the subdued Impressionism of John H. Twachtman and J. Alden Weir, in which pastel and watercolor also reflect the new colorist tendency. This drawing, although basically traditional in concept, nevertheless documents Newell's awareness of the "Impressionist," an oddity in American art terminology of the time. It also serves to anticipate his evolving artistic maturity in the years just ahead.

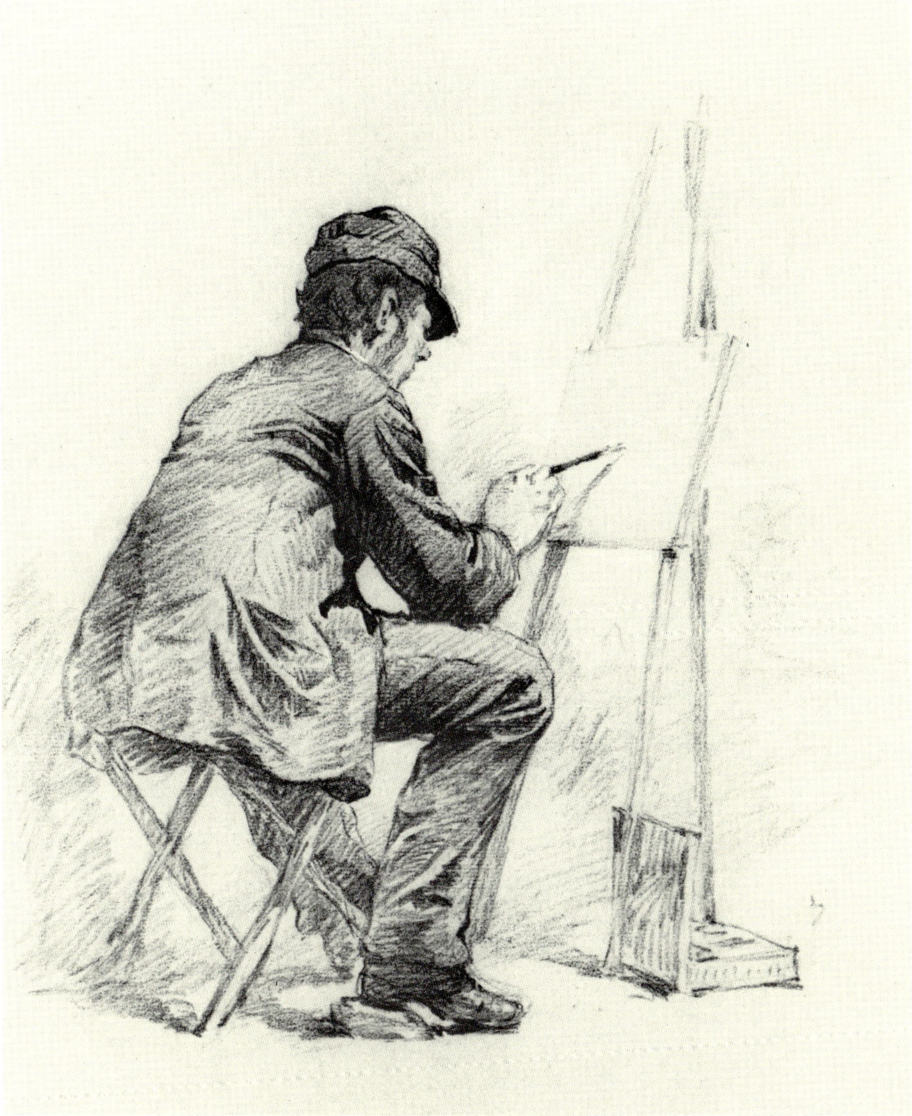

NO. 26 GILBERT STUART NEWTON (1794-1835)

Portrait of a Young Girl, ca. 1825
Black and red chalk, heightened with white, on buff paper ; 7 5/8 x 5 3/4 in.

Signed in ink, lower right: G.S. Newton

Newton was born in Halifax, Nova Scotia, but was brought up in Charleston, near Boston, by his widowed mother, a sister of the artist Gilbert Stuart. When Stuart opened a studio in Boston, young Newton received his first instruction in painting from his famous uncle and namesake. The relationship was of short duration, however, and he soon afterward decided to go abroad to Italy and France to continue his studies. Newton's chance meeting in Paris with Charles Robert Leslie, an English artist his own age, who also had close family connections in America, encouraged him to accompany Leslie to England to seek his fortune. Like Leslie, he was soon to earn a considerable reputation in London as a painter of literary and historical subjects, Newton becoming noted particularly for his facility in painting and innate sense of color. His earliest English manner shows some influence in choice of color and technique from a brief association with Washington Allston in London. His more mature painting and drawing styles, as seen in this drawing, indicates a clear inspiration from Watteau, whose drawings in the *trois crayons* manner he would have recalled chiefly from his Paris days.

In time, Newton preferred to regard himself as an English painter but, still within his lifetime, Dunlap was the first historian to claim him as an American artist. Dunlap also characterized Newton as a pupil of Benjamin West, but any direct contact with West in his last years seems highly unlikely. The relationship with West, if any, would have been somewhat remote, probably through Allston and Leslie.

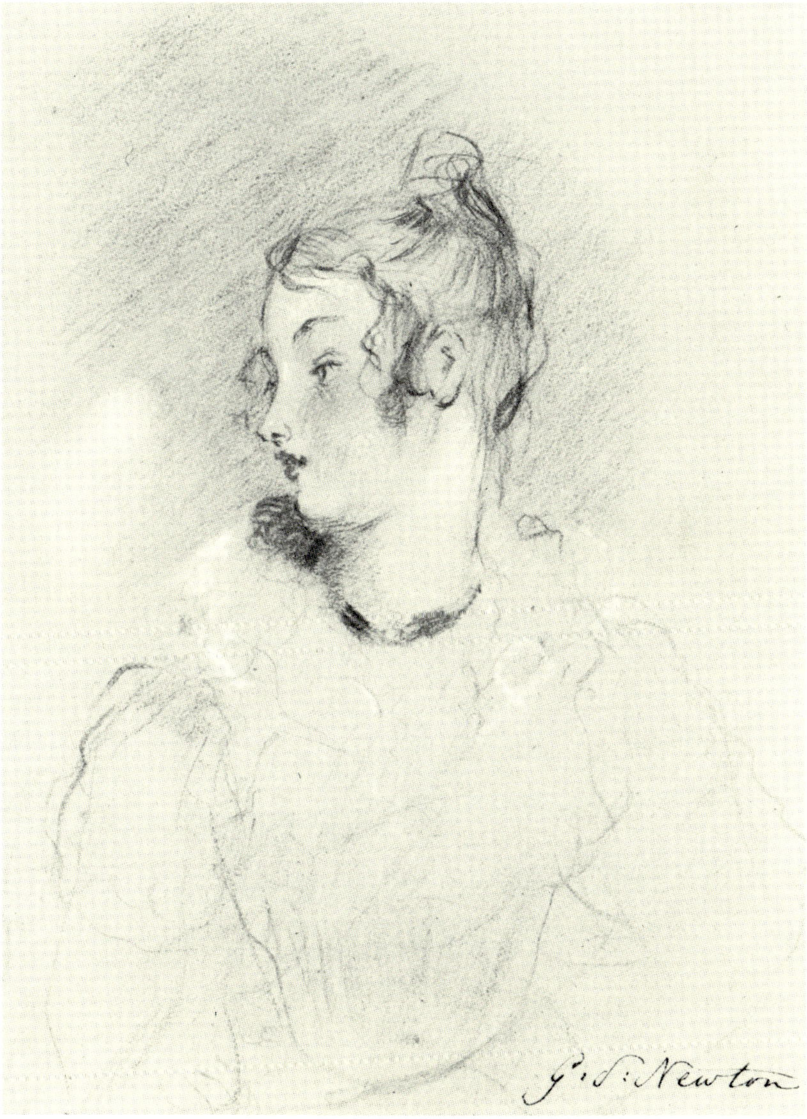
G. S. Newton

NO. 27 JOHANNES ADAM SIMON OERTEL (1823-1909)

Portrait of an Elderly Man, 1883
Charcoal on tan paper; 8 3/8 x 7 in.

Signed lower right: J.A. Oertel

Prov: The artist; Charles Lanman, Georgetown, D.C.

Oertel was a painter of religious and portrait subjects, as well as an Episcopal clergyman. Born in Germany, he was trained in Munich before coming to America in 1848 and settling in Newark, New Jersey. He taught drawing, engraved banknotes, and was responsible for some of the ceiling decorations in the House of Representatives in 1857/1858. During the Civil War he served with the Army of the Potomac. From 1871 until his retirement in 1895 he became a priest of the Protestant Episcopal Church and served many parishes, chiefly in the south. After 1895 he devoted himself to a series of religious pictures, the most important being his work for the National Cathedral in Washington.

Charles Lanman's collection included paintings and drawings by the artist. A strong supporter of Oertel, Lanman kept a running correspondence with him on art and personal matters for more than thirty years. In 1889 Lanman prepared a biographical account of Oertel's life and work (unpublished) which he planned to include in a revised edition of his *Random Recollections*. Five years earlier, Lanman sent a letter to the Washington *Sunday Post* with reference to Oertel: "It is now about 20 years since I expressed the opinion that, in the higher characteristics of art, Mr. Oertel was without a peer in the United States, and that opinion remains unchanged. It was founded on his rare abilities as a draftsman; his consummate knowledge of the human form; his powers of grouping figures in large numbers and thereby depicting ideal scenes teeming with thought and instruction, and his thorough knowledge of color. His skill in portraiture is also unusual. . . ." This highly finished portrait drawing, which the artist presented to Lanman shortly before the *Sunday Post* letter was published, may have been intended to demonstrate the specific aspects of draftsmanship and "skill in portraiture" Lanman afterward referred to.

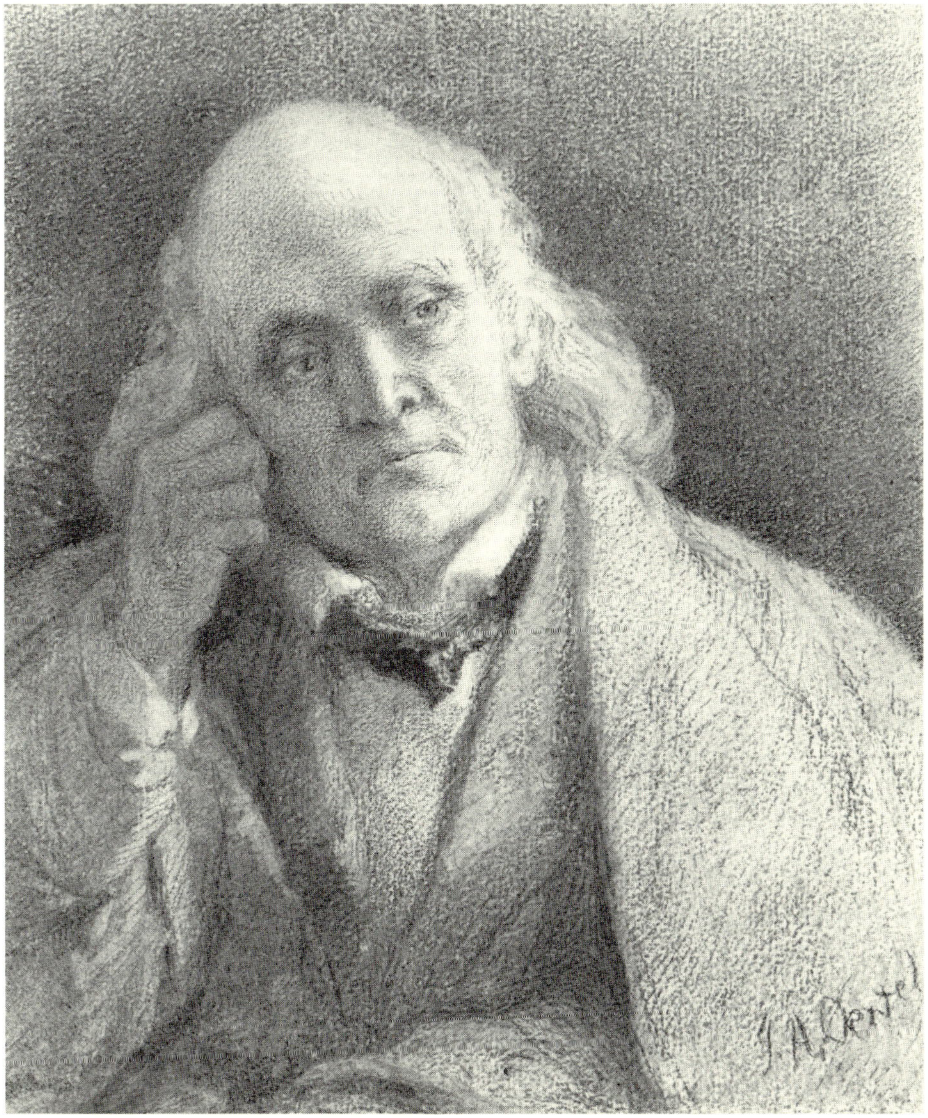

NO. 28 WILLIAM TYLEE RANNEY (1813-1845)

Frontier Horse auction, ca. 1845
Recto and verso: Pencil on cream paper; 8 3/4 x 11 5/8 in.

A double-sided drawing. Verso: sketch of "Gist rescuing Washington from the Allegheny River."

Exh: William Ranney, Painter of the Early West (Washington, D.C., The Corcoran Gallery of Art, 1962), nos. 132, 133 (illus.); *American Genre Painting in the Victorian Era* (New York, Hirschl & Adler Galleries, 1978), no. 66.

Prov: Estate of the artist; grandson, Claude J. Ranney, Malvern, Pennsylvania; Hirschl & Adler Galleries, New York.

Ranney was not only a close contemporary of George Caleb Bingham but also, like him, one of the first American narrative painters to devote himself to subjects of western frontier life and history. There are, in fact, distinct parallels between the two artists in background and experience, but Ranney's evolving career was cut short by his untimely death. His early contact in Texas with trappers, hunters, and mountain men provided the subject matter that he preferred and on which his fame rests. Ranney actually called New York, and ultimately Hoboken, New Jersey, his home. He was elected an Associate Member of the National Academy in 1850 and exhibited at the Academy as early as 1838. Like Bingham, he submitted his first picture to the American Art-Union in 1845 and continued to seek the organization's patronage until its demise seven years later. This drawing is, in all probability, a finished study for a proposed painting. The slight sketch on the verso is one of two extant drawings related to a painting of "Washington and Gist Crossing the Allegheny River" which Ranney painted in 1854.

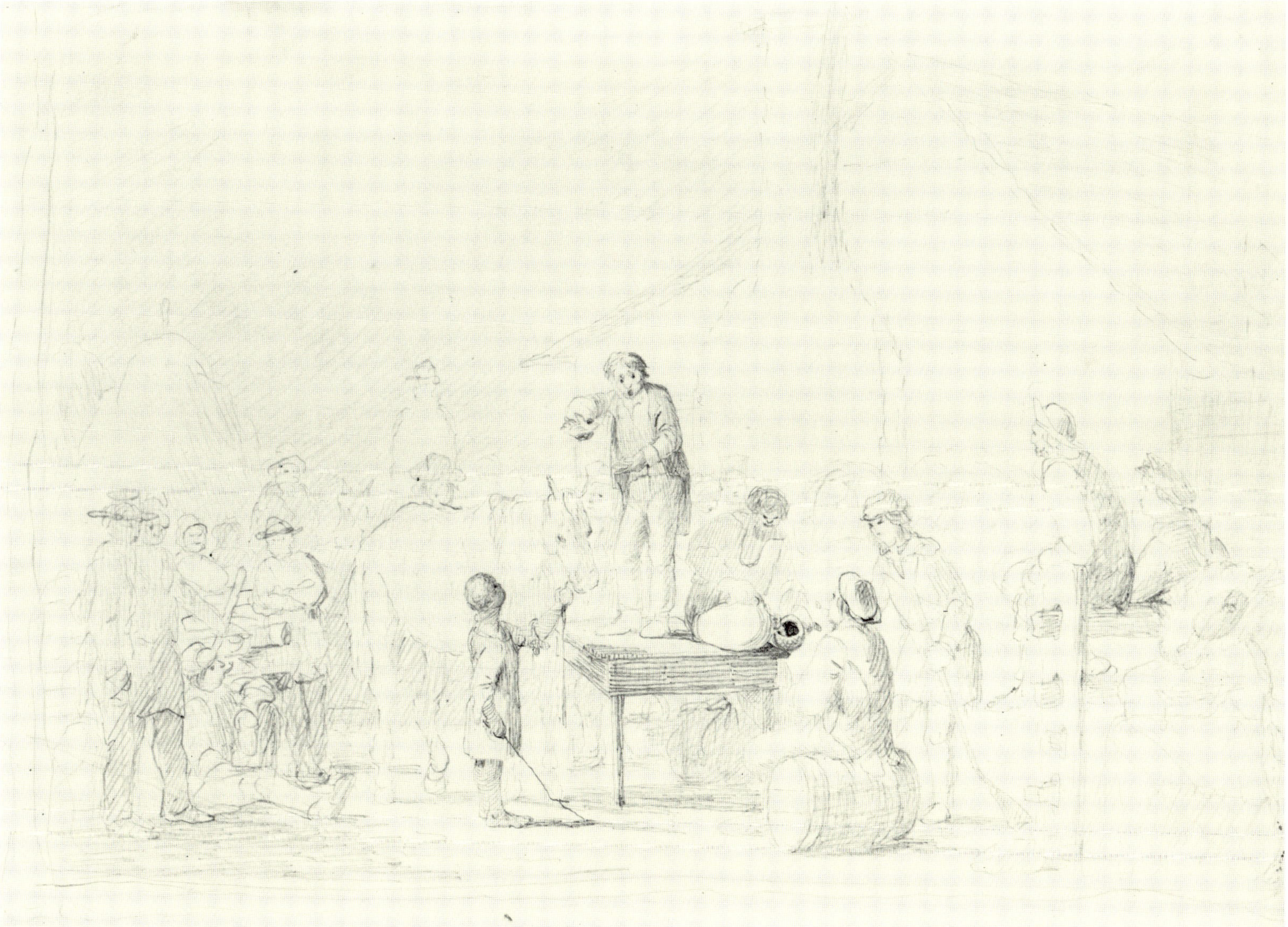

NO. 29 TOBY EDWARD ROSENTHAL (1848-1917)

Sheet of Sketches, ca. 1870
Pencil on tan paper; 10 5/8 x 15 1/4 in.

Signed, initials, on bench, left. Inscribed: Rosen/thal, lower right, probably by another hand. A double-sided sheet with additional sketches, verso.

Rosenthal was born in Germany and brought to America in 1853 when his family emigrated and settled first in New Haven and soon after in San Francisco, where he began his art studies. By 1864 he was working under the direction of perhaps the best-known California artist of the day, Fortunato Arriola, who was to become his close friend and mentor. Although, at seventeen, he had already gained a reputation at home, it was Arriola who encouraged Rosenthal's father to find the support necessary to send him abroad in 1866. The goal was Munich where he ultimately became a pupil of Karl von Piloty at the Academy. Despite strong family ties at home, Rosenthal decided by 1872 to remain permanently in Munich. Although he always considered himself an American artist, and a Californian in particular, he found the artistic climate in Munich more favorable to what he hoped to achieve in his chosen field. This drawing dates unquestionably from his Munich period, but it reflects the healthy respect for correct drawing he learned from his earlier studies in America.

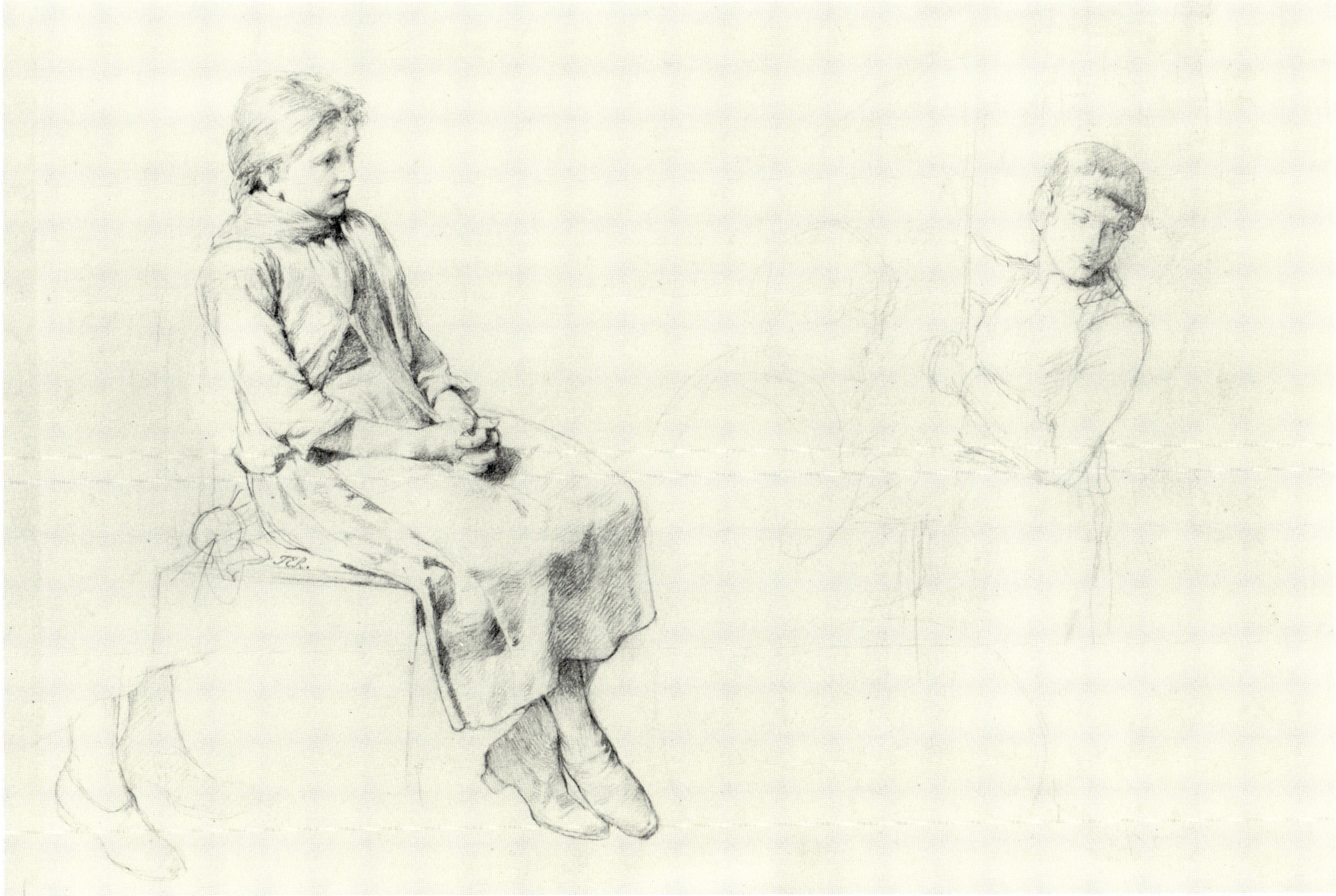

NO. 30 CHARLES BALTHAZAR JULIEN FEVRET DE SAINT-MÉMIN (1770-1852)

Portrait of a Gentleman, ca. 1803/1810
Black crayon, heightened with white chalk, on tinted pink paper; 19 1/2 x 13 3/4 in. (sight)

Prov: Henry Francis duPont, Winterthur, Delaware; H.F. duPont Winterthur Museum, 1978; Auction, Sotheby's New York, April 28, 1978, lot 31; Auction, Sotheby's New York, Jan. 29, 1988, lot 1145.

Saint-Mémin was born in France, destined for a military career that was to change abruptly with the Revolution. His family fled the country, finally arriving in America, where they settled at first in New York in 1793. Seeking a means of supporting his family, he was encouraged to use his talent for drawing by learning to engrave city landscapes and then merchandise the impressions. A second means was to design and construct a mechanical device called a physionotrace which enabled him to trace an accurate profile portrait. He added the modeling and detail to produce an effective likeness. Saint-Mémin supplied his client with a life-size "crayon" on tinted pink paper, displayed in a gilt frame with an octagonal black mat on glass decorated in gold. It also included a copper plate with the drawing reduced by the aid of a pantograph and engraved, together with twelve proofs. The total cost was thirty-three dollars for the male portraits, slightly more for the women. It became his main source of income for the twenty years he was to spend in this country. With headquarters first in New York, later in Philadelphia and Burlington, New Jersey, Saint-Mémin was for a brief time assisted by partners, Thomas Bluget de Valdenuit and Louis Le Met (or Lemet); however, by far the largest production of portraits—at least 818—was due to him. After working in New York and Philadelphia, Saint-Mémin traveled south to Baltimore, Annapolis, and Washington, then to Alexandria, Richmond, and elsewhere in Virginia. During a short stay in Charleston, it was reported that fashionable society crowded his establishment. Saint-Mémin visited France again in 1810-12, then decided to return permanently to his native Dijon in 1814. He became director of the town's Municipal Museum in 1817. This drawing, probably of a southern gentleman, shows a bold use of the graphic medium that goes beyond a mechanical aid to effect an elegant, sensitive, and lively image. Since the subject is not identified in lists of Saint-Mémin's engravings, we can assume the order was only for the "crayon."

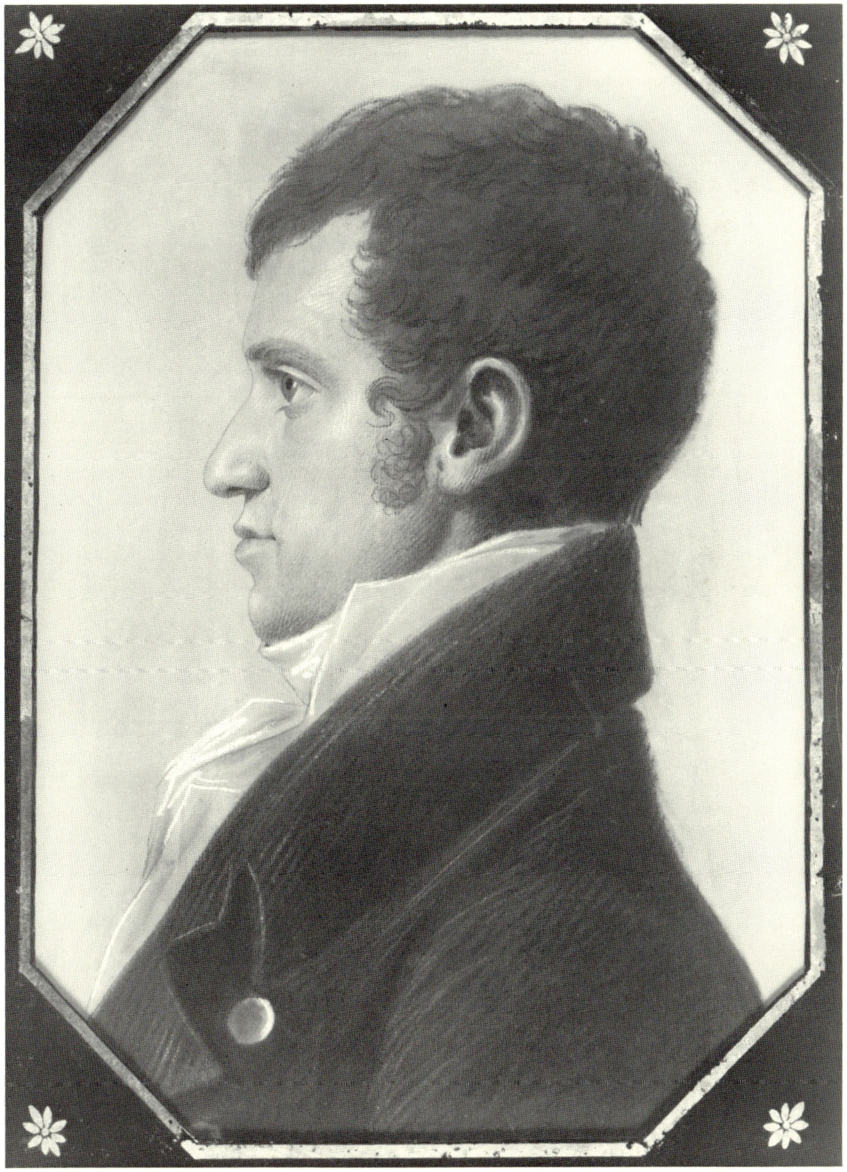

NO. 31 JULES EMILE SAINTIN (1829-1894)

A. *Portrait of Millard Fillmore, 1856*
Pencil and sgraffito on gesso paper;
5¾ x 4½ in. (oval)

Signed and dated, lower center: J. Emile Saintin New York 1856; inscribed above: Hon. E. Fillmore Vice President of the U.S./ of New York

B. *Portrait of Washington Irving, 1859*
Pencil and sgraffito on gesso paper;
3⅝ x 2¾ in. (oval)

Signed and dated, lower right: J.E. Saintin/ 1859 New York; inscribed below: Washington Irving of New York x 1859

C. *Portrait of John Charles Frémont, 1856*
Pencil and sgraffito on gesso paper;
5¾ x 4½ in. (oval)

Signed and dated, lower center: J.Emile Saintin New York 1856; inscribed above: Colonel Fremont of New York

Exh: The French in America (Detroit Institute of Arts, 1951) nos. 495-497

Saintin was born in France and studied in Paris at the Ecole des Beaux Arts, working chiefly under Drolling. A prolific artist in oil, pastel, crayon, and pencil, he exhibited at the Paris Salons from 1848 to 1882 where he became best known for a series of paintings of sentimental genre. His most significant work was probably accomplished during the ten years he spent in the United States (1853-1863). Settling in New York, his work included scenes of the city streets, dramatic studies of American Indians, and portraits of prominent people. After his return to France in 1863 he won medals at the Paris Salons of 1866 and 1870 and was represented in the French section at the Centennial Exhibition held in Philadelphia in 1876. In America, he exhibited earlier at the Boston Athenaeum , the Brooklyn Art Association, and the National Academy of Design, where he was elected an Associate Member in 1858.

Although these drawings were portraits of contemporary subjects, it seems likely that none of those now extant —which also include portraits of Abraham Lincoln, Stephen A. Douglas, and John Brown (not in exhibition)—were made from life. The technique, involving pencil on tinted papers over a gesso ground which was scratched through to produce the highlights, seems to have been used by relatively few artists. Since erasures and corrections were not possible, this was obviously a technique that would discourage all but the surest draftsmen.

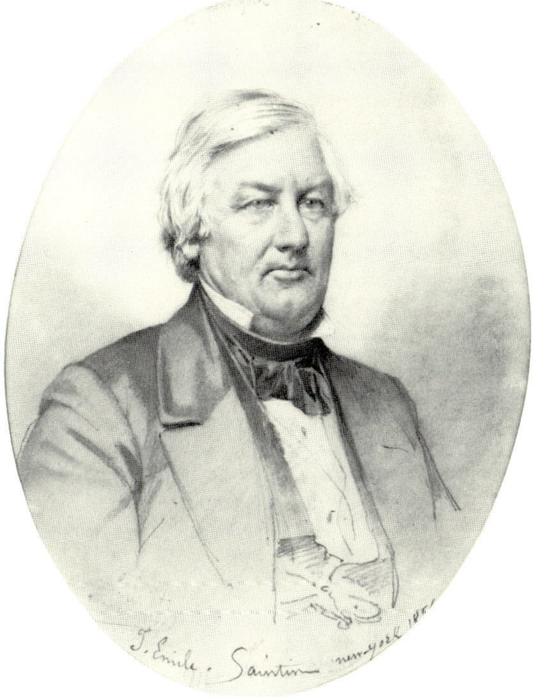

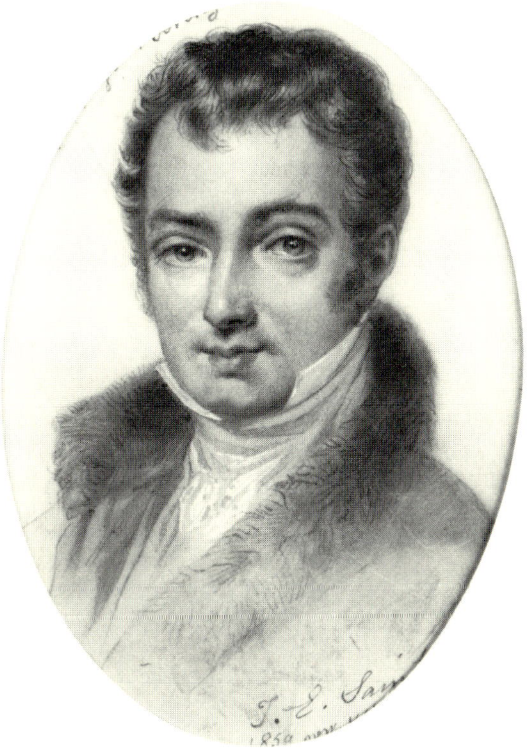

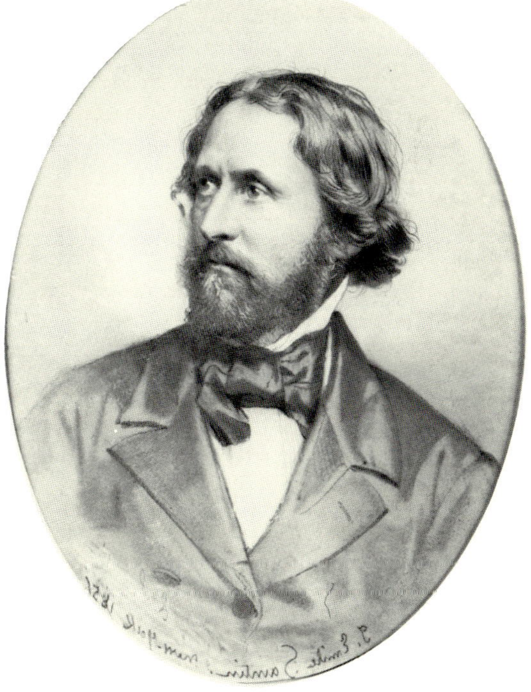

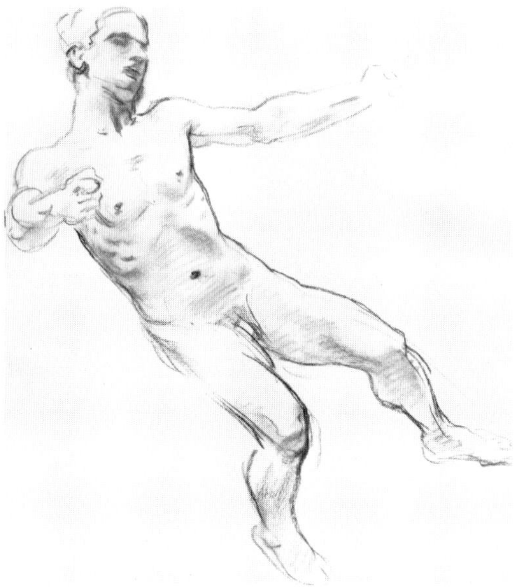

NO. 32 JOHN SINGER SARGENT (1856-1925)

Study for* Gassed, *1918/1919
Charcoal and stump on beige laid paper watermarked MICHALLET/FRANCE; 18 3/4 x 24 3/8 in.

Inscribed, obverse, lower right: 17.2.2 XII(?) S.4.49; verso, upper right: S.4.49. A double-sided drawing. Verso: Sketch of a Falling Male Nude

Exh: Images of the Great War: 1914-1918 (University of California, Los Angeles, Grunwald Center, 1983), no. 64.

Prov: Estate of the artist; Miss Emily Sargent and Mrs. Violet Sargent Ormond; The Corcoran Gallery of Art, Washington, D.C., until 1961.

In the spring of 1918 Sargent was commissioned by the British Ministry of Information to go to the Western Front to observe and record war scenes that would be of historic value, but more specifically to produce a painting dealing with British and American cooperation. Although advanced in age, with no previous experience in battle painting, Sargent felt that he could not refuse the invitation. He went to France late in June, and immediately upon his arrival began to fill his notebooks with sketches of soldier types and of the troops in trenches. Sargent's major painting, *Gassed* (90 1/2 x 240 in.; Imperial War Museum, London) is based on an event he witnessed on August 21, 1918 when he visited the casualty station at La Bac-de-Sud on the Arras-Doullens road and saw the arrival of men who had been gassed that day. The sketches he made on the spot of the blinded soldiers inspired and formed the basis of the essentially medical theme Sargent elected to use for the painting. This drawing is clearly a preliminary study produced in his London studio for the group of three figures from left to center of the classical frieze-like composition.

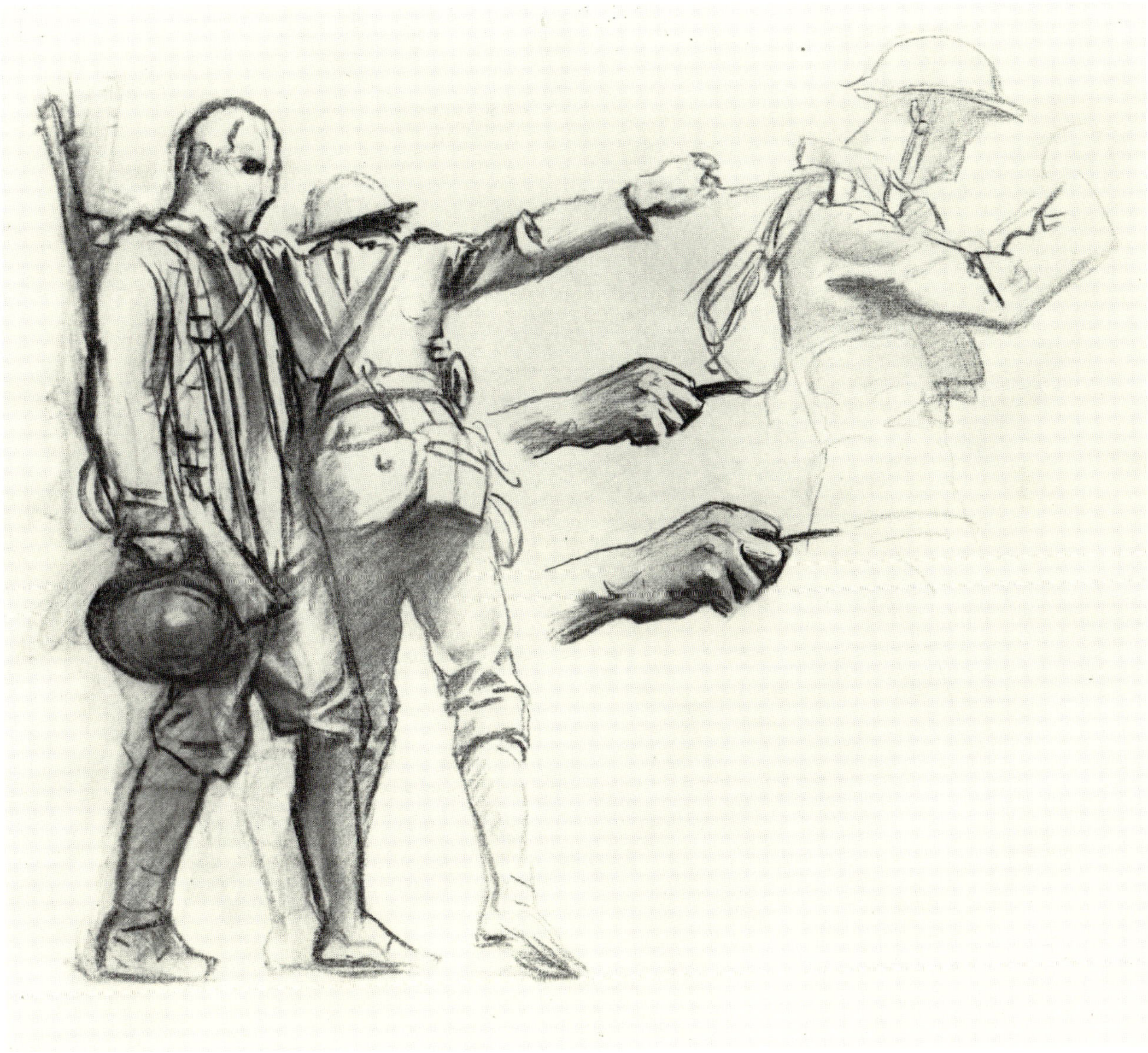

NO. 33 NAPOLEON SARONY (1821-1896)

Seated Woman in Oriental Costume
Charcoal and white chalk on gray paper; 16 1/16 x 10 3/4 in.

Signed lower right: Sarony

Sarony was born in Quebec and came to New York about 1836 where he studied drawing under a drawing master (probably Alexander Robertson). He later worked as a lithographer for Nathaniel Currier and Henry R. Robinson. By 1846 he formed a partnership in the lithographic publishing business with Henry B. Major, the firm of Sarony & Major continuing until 1857 when George K. Knapp became associated with them. Sarony himself retired from the firm in 1867 in order to travel abroad. After six years spent chiefly in Europe, he returned to New York, but soon left for England to start what was to become a most successful career as a professional photographer. When he eventually returned to New York to open a studio, his name soon became synonymous with fine portrait photography. Later in life Sarony also became known for his charcoal portraits and for the decorative drawings of nude and lightly clad female figures that reflected French academic taste of the time. A colorful figure in appearance and dress, Sarony was nonetheless a serious craftsman and an artist who exhibited at the National Academy and elsewhere to the last years of his life.

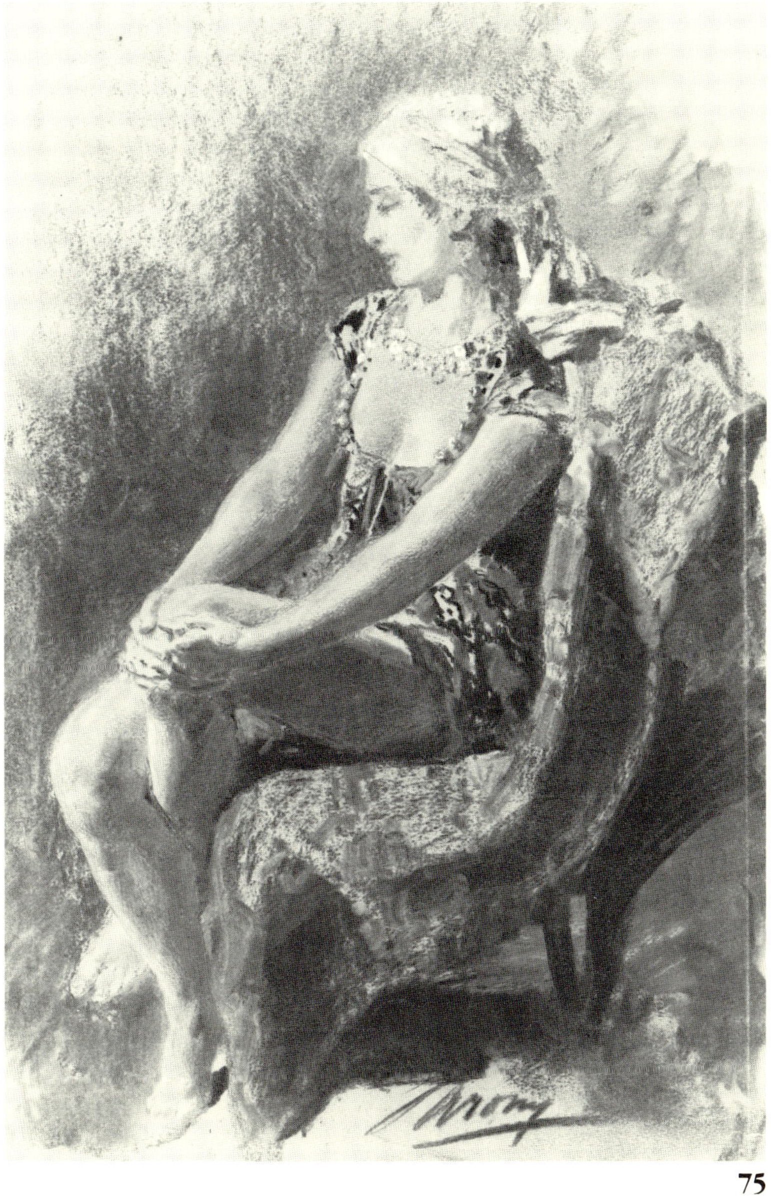

NO. 34 CHRISTIAN SCHUSSELE (1824/26-1879)

The Homecoming, 1863
Gray wash over pencil on Bristol board;
12 1/4 x 9 1/4 in.(framing line)

Signed and dated in ink, lower left:
C. Schussele/63

Schussele was born in Alsace, the son of a baker. He first studied drawing and lithography at the Strasbourg Academy before going to Paris in 1843 to continue his studies in art under Delaroche and Yvon. The Revolution of 1848 cut short his studies and prompted his emigration to America. Settling in Philadelphia, he supported himself as a lithographer, designer of banknotes, and illustrator for magazines and books. Following the favorable reception of one of his paintings in 1854 he felt encouraged to devote himself to a career as a painter of history, genre, and landscape. He began to exhibit regularly at the Pennsylvania Academy, but was compelled to curtail his burgeoning career when he developed a palsy condition in his right hand. From 1865 to 1868 he traveled in Europe in search of an effective treatment, but to no avail. On his return he was offered and accepted the post of professor of drawing at the Pennsylvania Academy, a position he was to occupy for the rest of his life.

This drawing typifies a sentimental genre which Schussele and Darley, among others, made popular in paintings and illustration during the Civil War period. The precise draftsmanship and technique reflects Schussele's academic training abroad that also characterizes the impact European style and method had on the teaching of drawing in America well into the second half of the nineteenth century.

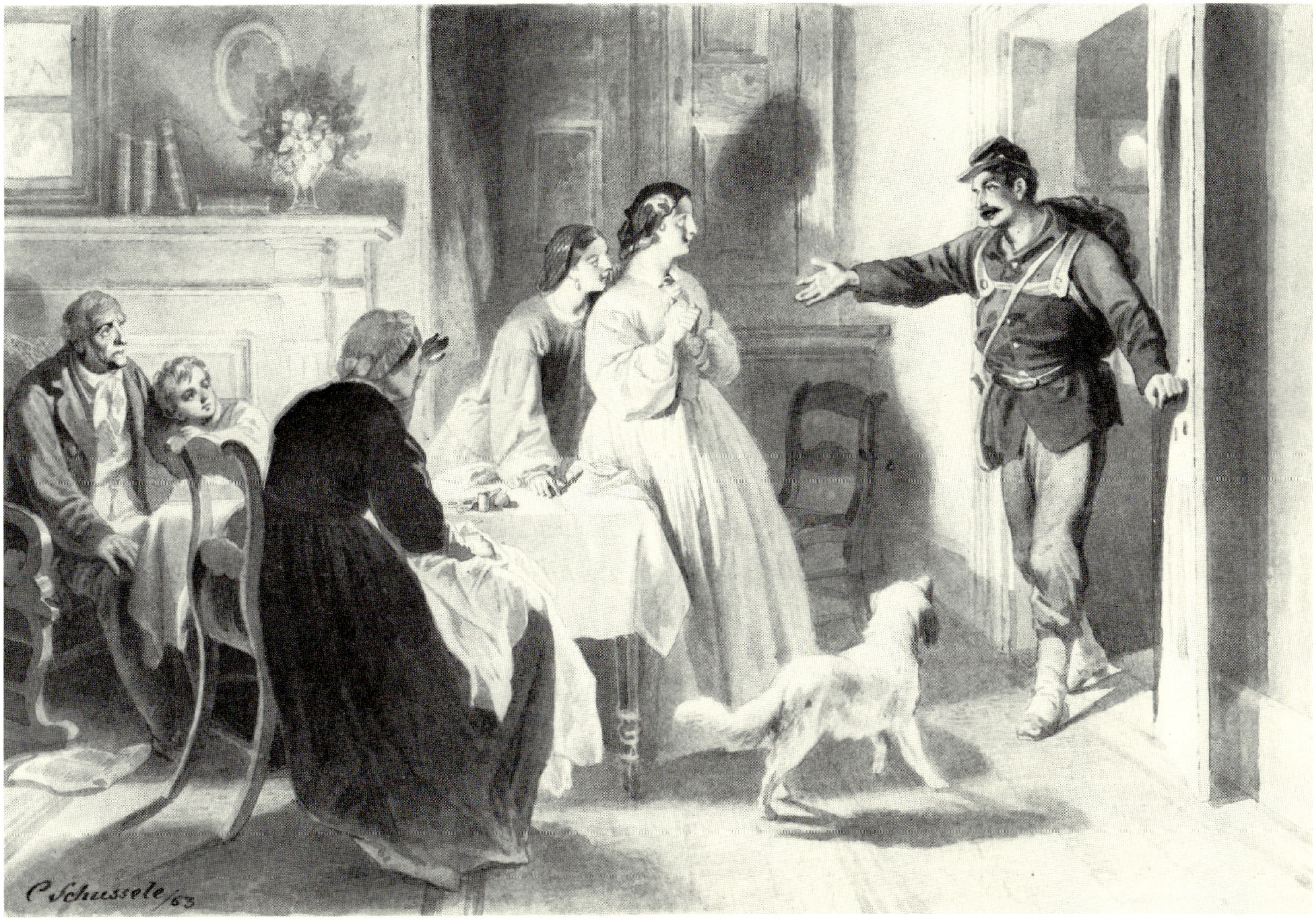
C Schussele/63

NO. 35 LILLY MARTIN SPENCER (1822-1902)

Ophelia, ca. 1846/1848
Pencil; 19 1/4 x 15 in.

Signed and titled in ink below: Opelia [sic] L.M. Spencer.

Prov: Estate of the artist; to granddaughter, Mrs. Donald R. Gates, until 1970; Hirschl & Adler Galleries, New York; Terry De Lapp, Los Angeles, California.

Angélique Marie (called "Lilly") Martin, was born in England of French parentage. The family had emigrated first to England, then to America in 1830, settling in New York and soon afterward in Marietta, Ohio, where Martin received her earliest art training. By the time she was nineteen, local recognition of her talent was encouraging enough to persuade the father to take his daughter to Cincinnati to further her art studies and professional experience. By 1848, when Martin decided to move to New York, she had married Benjamin Rush Spencer, adopted the Spencer name professionally, and had begun to raise a family that eventually reached thirteen, seven living to maturity. She also realized that she would have to be the breadwinner of the family. Frequent exhibitions in institutions such as the National Academy in New York, Pennsylvania Academy of the Fine Arts in Philadelphia, the Boston Athenaeum, the Washington Art Association, as well as the Art Unions in New York, Philadelphia, and Cincinnati, were prompted as much by her desire to enhance her reputation as the constant need to merchandise her work. She encouraged publicity in the newspapers and magazines, and sold pictures to the print publishers who produced the lithographs that were widely distributed across the country. Spencer's impressive reputation was to rest for many years on the popular sentimental genre pictures of domestic scenes in which women, children, and dogs always played central roles.

This drawing reveals a deeper insight into Spencer's artistic character. A study of psychological expression, it reflects an interest in mental aberration which apparently dates from her Ohio years. In 1846 she reportedly visited an asylum for the insane in Columbus. A drawing in the so-called *Pedlar Sketchbook*, titled "Insanity," may have stemmed from that visit and inspired further studies in an area that recalls Géricault's earlier investigations of madness of which she could not have been aware at the time. Along the same line she was also attracted to Shakespearian subjects in which Elizabethan conventions of madness were projected on the stage in terms of melodrama. (Cf. also John Hamilton Mortimer [1741-1779], "Ophelia," from a series of twelve etchings of "Shakespearian Heads," first published in London in 1775-1776, and reprinted in the early nineteenth century.)

Several drawings of this kind, including two of Ophelia, reveal an interest that could have been further stimulated by her awareness of Edwin Forrest, the leading Shakespearian actor of the day. He owned a farm in Covington, Kentucky, across the river from Cincinnati, and enjoyed a reputation that was based on his highly emotive characterizations. It can be assumed that he performed in Cincinnati and that Spencer saw the plays before coming to New York.

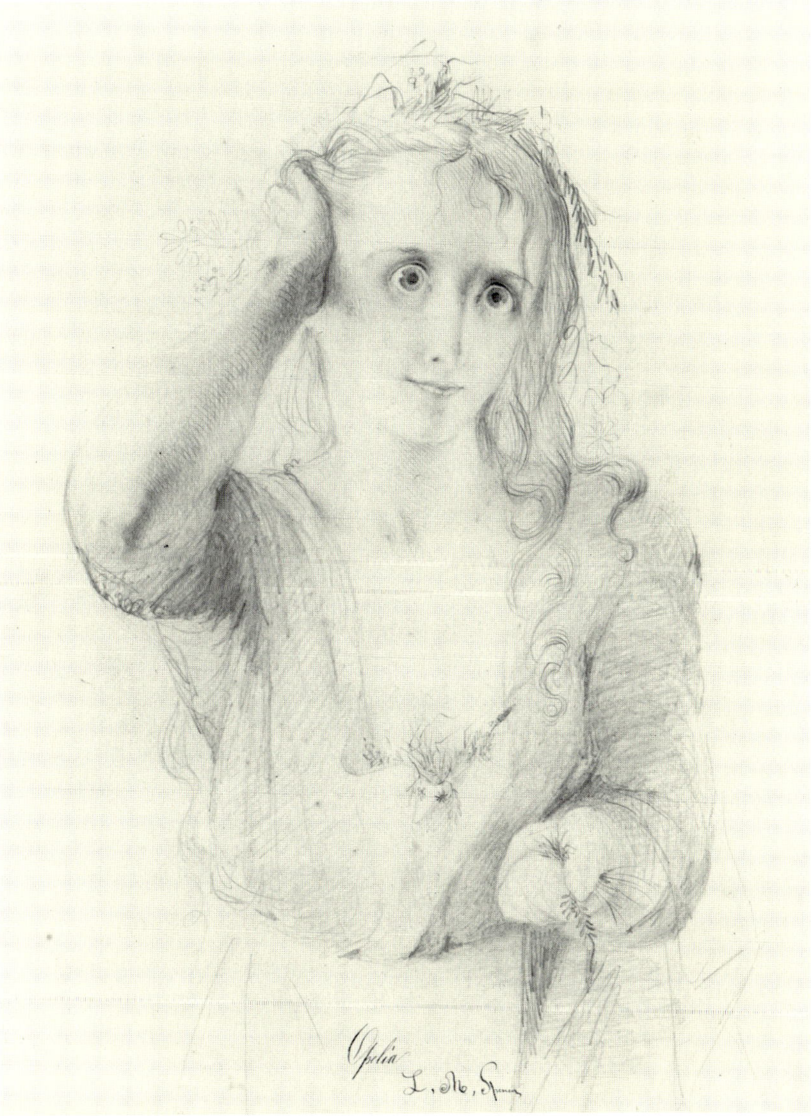

NO. 36 THOMAS SULLY (1783-1872)

Sheet of Six Figure Studies
Recto and verso: Pen and brown ink, gray wash, watercolor, on tan paper;
8 3/4 x 11 1/2 in.

Inscribed: color notations in pen beside three studies, recto; signature in pencil, lower right, by a later hand, verso.
A double-sided drawing. Verso: Seven figure studies.

Prov: Probably estate of the artist; Blanche Sully, artist's daughter; to her nephew, Frances Thomas Darley; Vincent Price, Los Angeles, California, 1937.

English born, Sully emigrated to America with his family, who settled in Charleston, South Carolina, in 1792. He credited Charles Fraser, a schoolmate, with being the first to instruct him in the rudiments of painting. Fraser, who afterward became a well-known miniature painter, apparently also introduced Sully to the art of miniature portraiture, as did his elder brother Lawrence Sully, with whom he lived in Richmond, Virginia, for several years. He was on his own by 1801, working as a miniaturist, but soon afterward began to paint portraits in oil. After beginning his professional career in New York in 1806, he went to Boston, where Gilbert Stuart gave him constructive criticism. He finally settled in Philadelphia but, still conscious of his need for more formal study, a friend persuaded seven art patrons to subsidize a trip to England. Once in London, an introduction to Benjamin West assured Sully the advantage of friendly criticism and free access to West's studio and collections. Other introductions led to visits to several of the best portrait painters of the day, including Sir Thomas Lawrence, whose elegant manner he sought to emulate upon his return to Philadelphia in 1810. By 1827 Sully had established himself as Philadelphia's foremost portrait painter, and not long afterward could claim a national fame that was to endure for the remainder of his long, productive life. The commission to paint a coronation portrait of the young Queen Victoria was unquestionably the highlight of his career, although Sully's reputation had been already established by

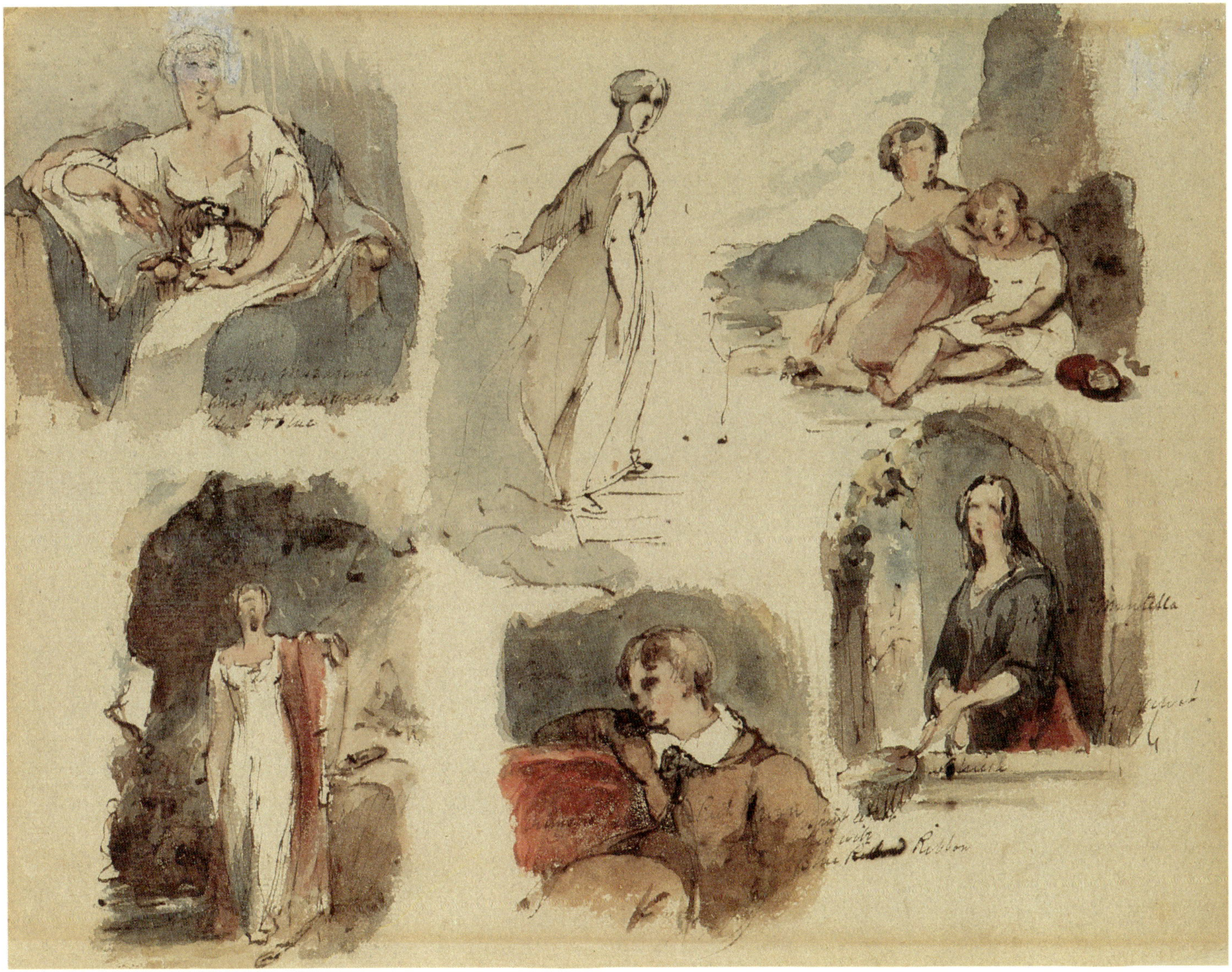

THOMAS SULLY
(Continued)

his monumental portrayals of Jefferson, Monroe, and Lafayette. But the return to England in fall of 1837 in the expectation of being able to paint the queen's portrait from life was obviously a special triumph.

Sully's vivid, pictorial style influenced and stimulated generations of aspiring American painters who saw the pictures he regularly contributed to the annual exhibitions of the National Academy, the Pennsylvania Academy, and the Boston Athenaeum, or came to know his work through the engravings that appeared in gift book annuals and elsewhere. Although he also occasionally accepted pupils, Sully, much like his mentor Benjamin West, evidently preferred to make himself readily accessible to the many young artists who sought his advice and criticism on a more informal basis.

This sheet of drawings is similar to the pages of the many sketchbooks Sully produced throughout his career, in which he made vignettes in pen, wash, and watercolor of ideas for future pictures. This page is unusual in its richness of color studies, and even more unusual in that the recto includes designs for two of the most important portraits he completed between 1838 and 1840, the full-lengths of Queen Victoria and Mrs. Reverdy Johnson. The sketch at the upper center, in pen and wash, is apparently a first idea for the composition he ultimately adopted for the queen's portrait, while that at lower left, in watercolor, is closely related to the preliminary oil study Sully made for the Johnson portrait, but altered considerably in the final version. In this instance, the contrast of the white dress with the red shawl dominates a color scheme Sully must have had in mind some time before the commission came his way. The verso, which includes a study for a three-quarter length male portrait, also shows sketches for several group portraits, as well as a "fancy subject" of the kind Sully was painting by the late 1830s.

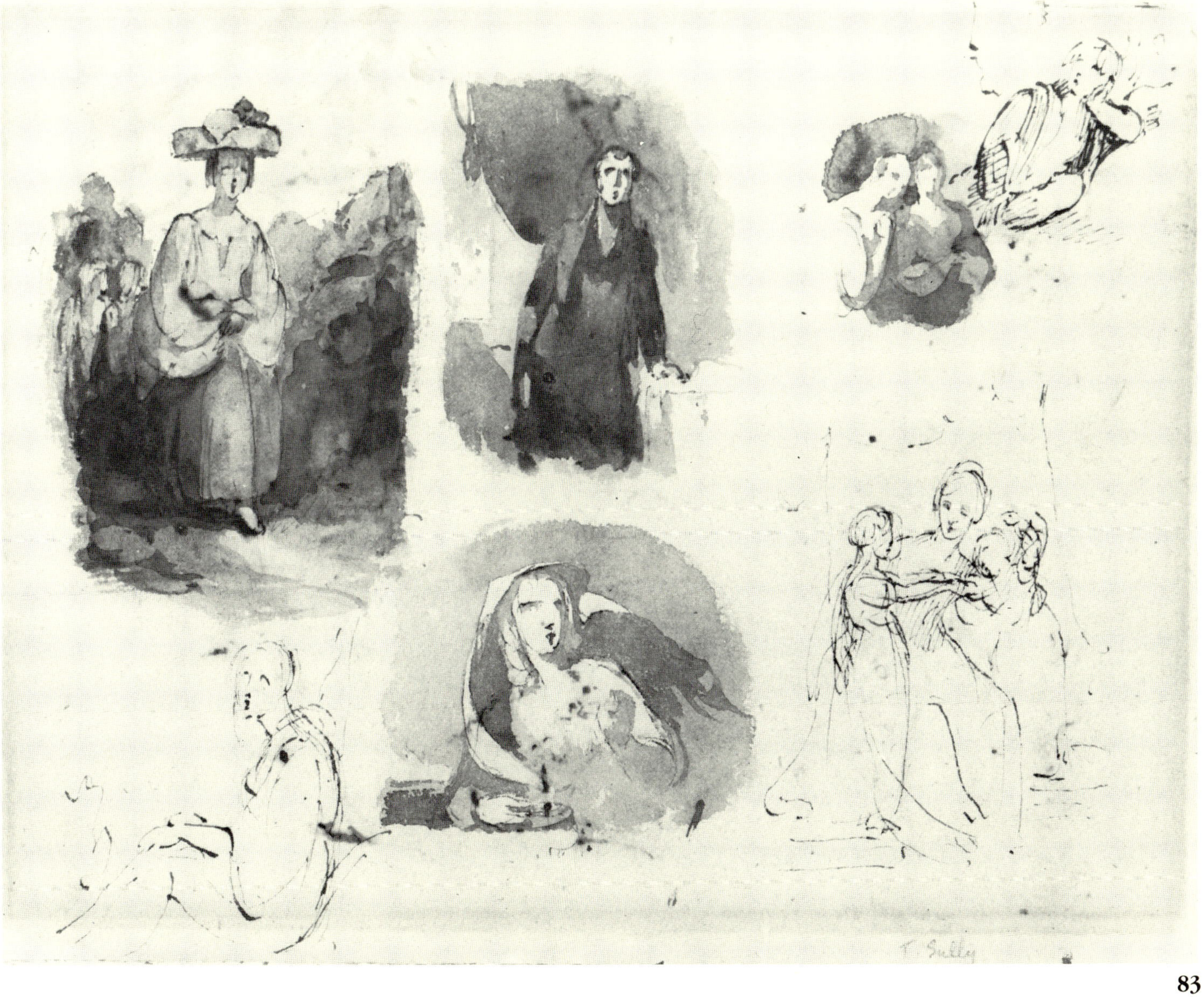
T. Sully

No. 37 Alfred Wordsworth Thompson (1840-1896)

Figure Studies, ca. 1870
Watercolor and pencil on gray paper;
7 x 9 3/4 in.

Thompson was born in Baltimore and educated there primarily with a law career in mind, but decided to become an artist shortly before the Civil War and opened a studio in Baltimore. During the first year of the conflict he served as a war illustrator for *Harper's Weekly*, but decided to go to France in 1861 for further study. In Paris he became a pupil of Glèyre and Barye and remained abroad until 1868. On his return he opened a studio in New York and began to exhibit regularly at the National Academy of Design. He was elected an Associate Member of the Academy in 1873 and a full Member two years afterward. Since Thompson subsequently made several sketching trips abroad, his subjects often included European landscape, although he is perhaps best known for his paintings of American life and history. This drawing, which may be among the "sketches from nature" Thompson exhibited at the Academy in 1871, also reflects the interest in the subjects of American life and history that established his reputation.

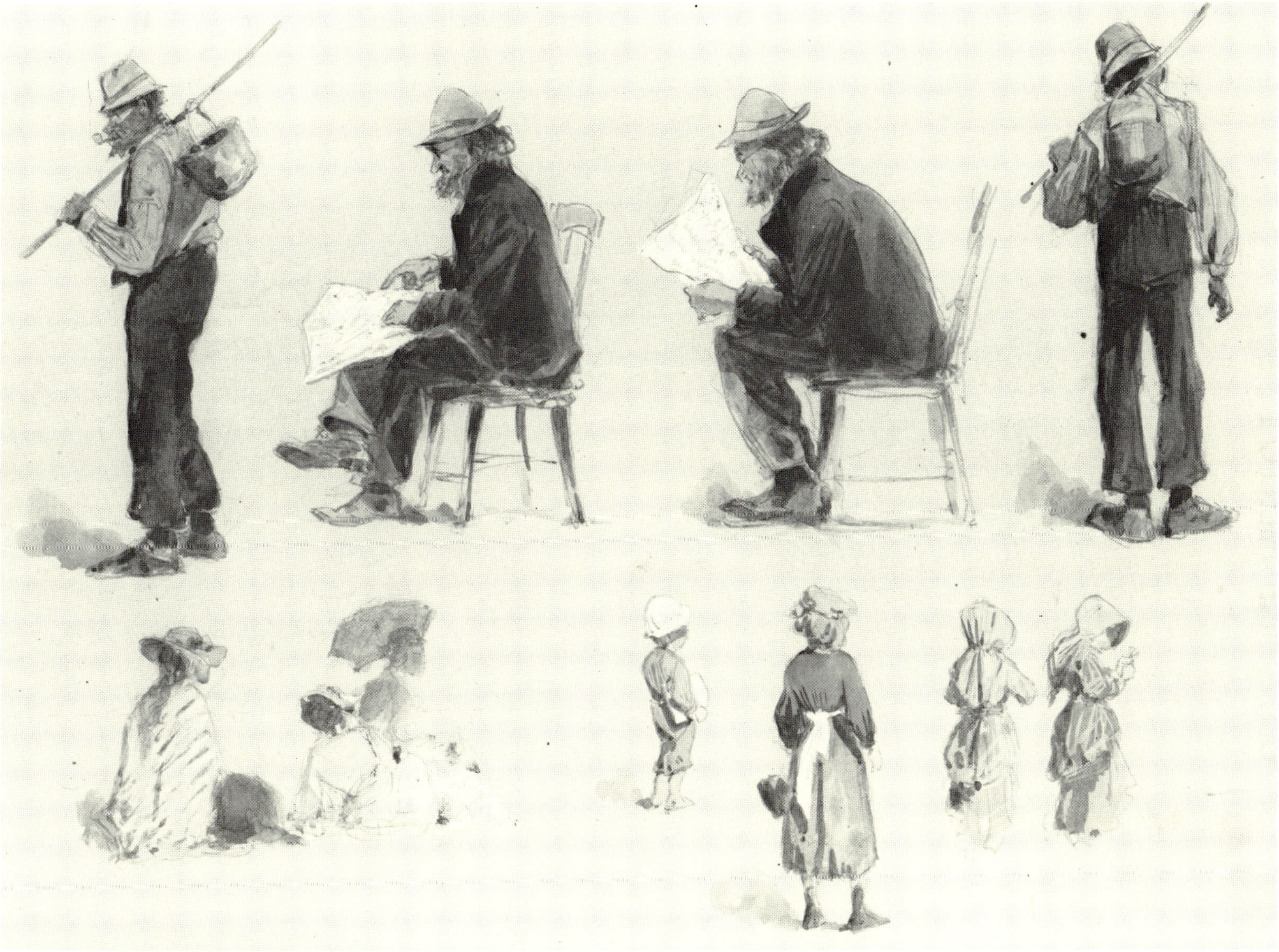

NO. 38 JOHN VANDERLYN (1775-1852)

Studies for* The Landing of Columbus, *early 1840s
Charcoal and white chalk on gray paper; 23 1/4 x 18 in.

Prov: Catherine Vanderlyn; to Judge A. Schoonmaker; to his daughter, Mrs. William Laughton; Fred Johnston; Kennedy Galleries, New York.

Vanderlyn was born in Kingston, New York, the grandson of the Dutch-born portrait painter, Pieter Vanderlyn (or Van Der Lyn), who had been active in Kingston, Albany, and Poughkeepsie during the first quarter of the eighteenth century. Sensing an inherited artistic talent, his family sent him to New York City in 1792, where he worked for a purveyor of artist's materials who also sold paintings and frames. While in New York he enrolled in the Columbian Academy of the Robertson brothers for instruction in drawing and design. A copy Vanderlyn made of a Gilbert Stuart portrait of the enterprising politician, Aaron Burr, led to a few months' apprenticeship with Stuart in Philadelphia, which was followed by Burr's support for further study in Paris in 1796. Armed with Burr's letters of recommendation to his influential friends abroad, Vanderlyn was made comfortable in his new surroundings and soon afterward admitted to the Ecole des Beaux-Arts where he began his studies under François André Vincent, a strict academician who provided discipline and an appreciation of the old masters.

Vanderlyn returned briefly to New York in 1801, but by 1803 went abroad again, this time remaining for twelve years, chiefly in Paris. When he was awarded a gold medal by Napoleon at the Paris Salon of 1808 for his history picture, *Marius on the Ruins of Carthage*, he firmly believed that his future as a painter of more than portraiture was assured. But when he returned to America in 1815, he found no ready acceptance for his major efforts. By that time his patron Burr was in disgrace and the American public was still unprepared to accept subjects like the nude *Ariadne* when the picture was placed on exhibition. A poor businessman, and an increasingly difficult personality, his various ventures failed along with the support of many of his colleagues.

Recognition of his ability as a history painter came some twenty-five years later when he was chosen over Samuel F. B. Morse to execute a painting for the Rotunda of the Capitol portraying *The Landing of Columbus*. Now a disheartened artist, reduced by poverty, Vanderlyn sought to refresh his spirit and energy by returning to Paris to carry out the important commission. Preparation for *Columbus* followed academic procedure. Vanderlyn made many drawings from nude models with extensive follow-up poses in full costume and detailed studies of significant features of individual figures. The major drawings were most certainly by Vanderlyn himself, although he is known to have delegated studies of costume details to an assistant, a not unusual procedure. This drawing, probably for the upraised arm of Columbus, is significant in that Columbus' gesture actually provides a focal point that also sets the mood for the composition. Vanderlyn's sensitive and incisive draftsmanship is still evident in the sheets of studies he made in preparation for the national commission. After so many years of neglect, Vanderlyn could obviously still find inspiration in the design and the message it was to convey, but no longer felt adequate to complete the monumental painting on his own and employed others of modest talent to assist him.

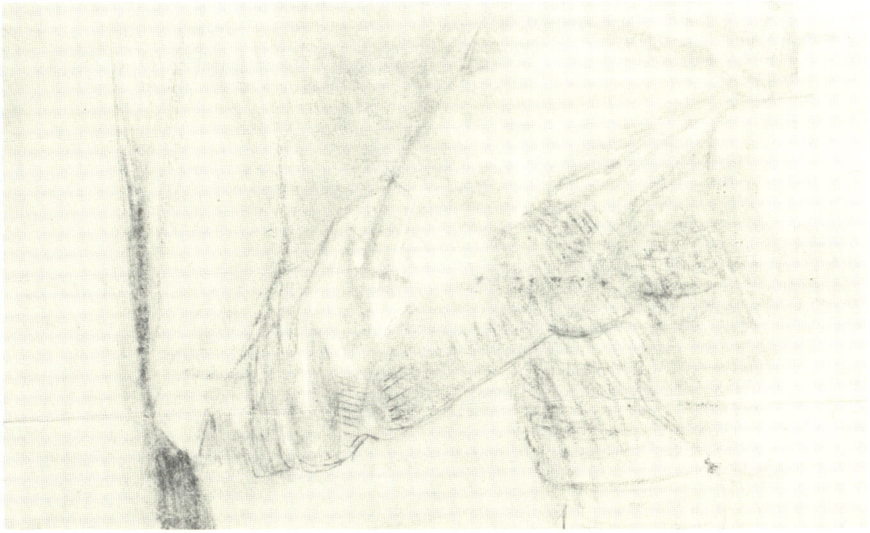

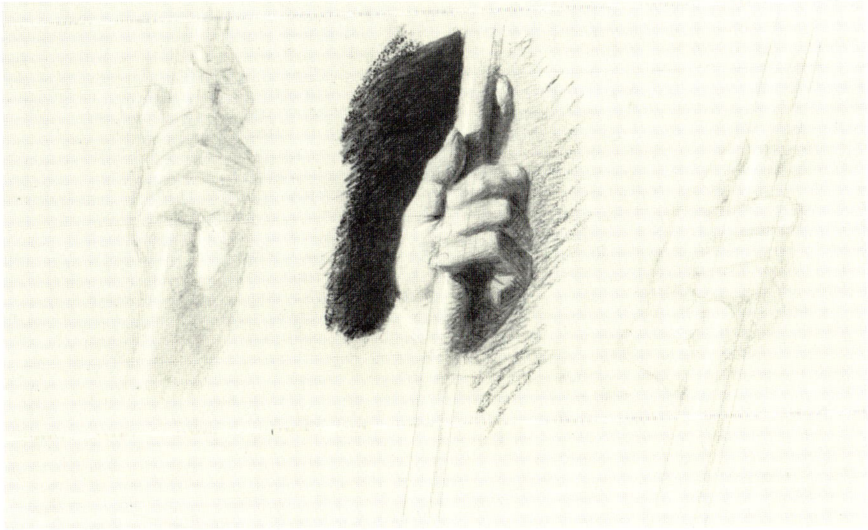

NO. 39 ELIHU VEDDER
(1836-1923)

***Study for* The Witch**
Black crayon and white chalk on gray paper; 9 1/2 x 6 1/4 in.

Prov: Estate of the artist; Victor D. Spark, New York.

Vedder was born in New York City, but spent his boyhood in upper New York state in Schenectady, where he first displayed a talent for drawing. He later received some formal instruction in Sherburne from Tompkins H. Matteson. In 1856 he went to Paris, where he studied in Picot's atelier before going to Italy. He returned to New York at the outbreak of the Civil War, but left for Italy again in 1865, this time settling permanently in Rome. From that vantage point he continued to exhibit at the National Academy, and to execute mural commissions for Bowdoin College, the Library of Congress, and the Collis P. Huntington residence in New York. His designs for the *Rubaijat of Omar Khayyam* (1884) also made him famous as a book illustrator. Vedder can be related to a number of other American figure painters of his time, like Kenyon Cox and Will Low, although he used classical form to express mystical ideas that indicate a more individual expression. As an artist-illustrator alone, drawing assumes a major role in his work, but the richness and variety of his technical prowess extends into all other areas of his graphic accomplishment. In this preparatory drawing, all distracting detail has been stripped away to focus attention on the haunting, abstract beauty of a favorite model.

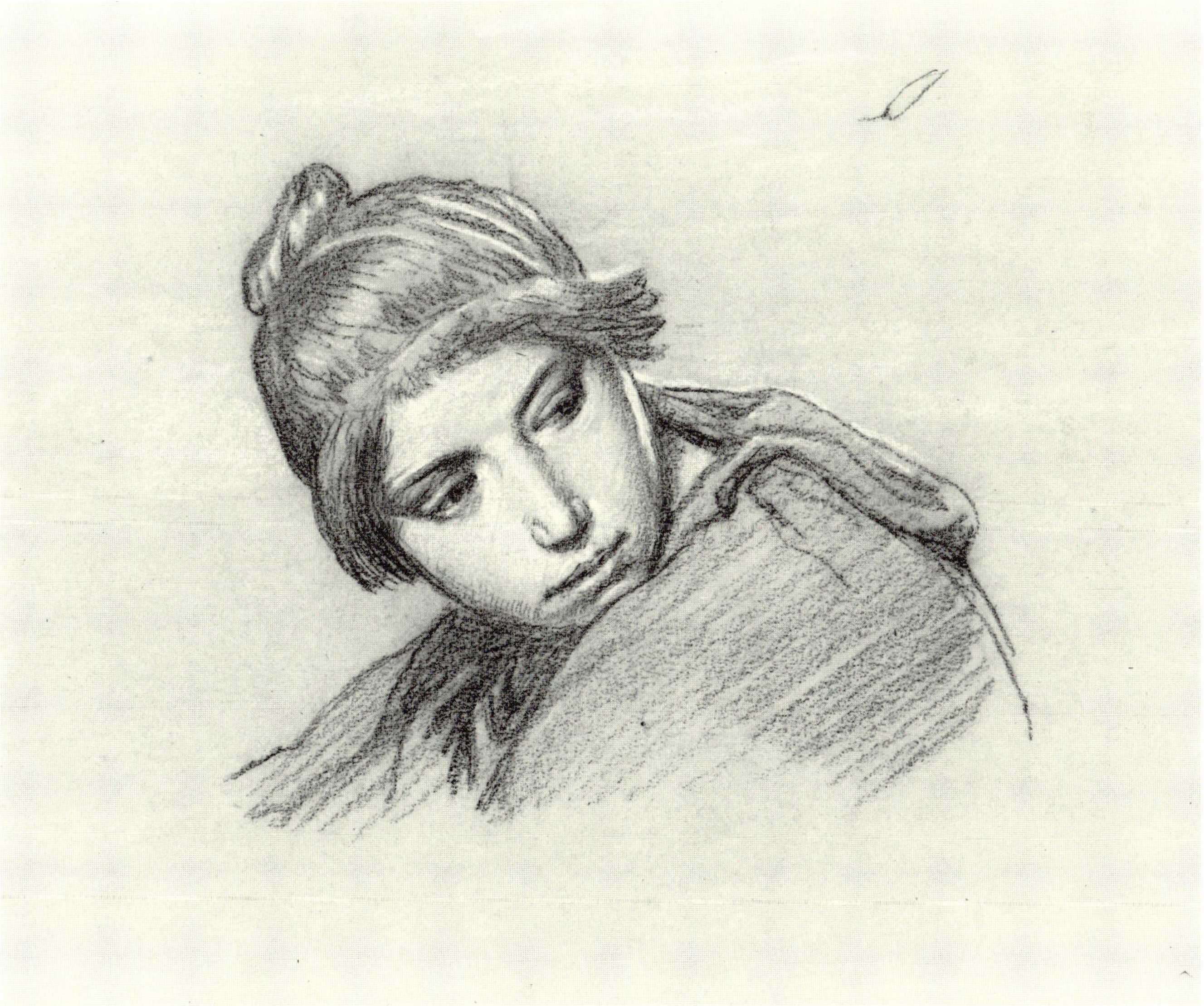

NO. 40 ALFRED RUDOLPH WAUD (1828-1891)

"Rebs" in the Bullpen, Brandy Station, 1863

Black crayon, heightened with white, on tan paper; 7 3/8 x 8 1/2 in.

Signed lower left: A.R. Waud; inscribed lower right: "Rebs" in the bullpen Brandy Station/1863

Waud was born in London, England, and studied art at both Somerset House and the Royal Academy before emigrating to the United States about 1858. He supported himself at first by theater scene painting in New York, but soon moved to Boston where he learned how to sketch directly on the woodblock for subsequent engraving. This experience prepared him for a career in illustration and he soon found work in the field for the *New York Illustrated News.* He was to achieve his most enduring fame as a Civil War artist-correspondent for *Harper's Weekly* and saw considerable action with the Army of the Potomac. Waud, his brother William, and Theodore Russell Davis were among the best of the illustrators in the field during the conflict and their work continued to be in demand for publication long after the war ended. After the war, *Harper's* sent Waud and Davis on an illustrating tour of the west; then Waud traveled through the south and southwest for *Every Saturday*. After his unexpected death in Marietta, Georgia, his drawings were acquired by J. Pierpont Morgan for the Library of Congress. The actual Civil War field sketches also survive, along with the highly finished gouaches he produced in the 1880s for publications like *Battles and Leaders of the Civil War.* This drawing seems not to have been published, but most probably was intended as an autonomous design for presentation or exhibition. Brandy Station, Virginia, was the headquarters of the Army of the Potomac. A confederate advance was made in that area August 20, 1862. A battle also took place at Brandy Station on June 9, 1863, regarded as the first great calvary action of the war. The sketch most likely represents the Confederate prisoners taken at that time.

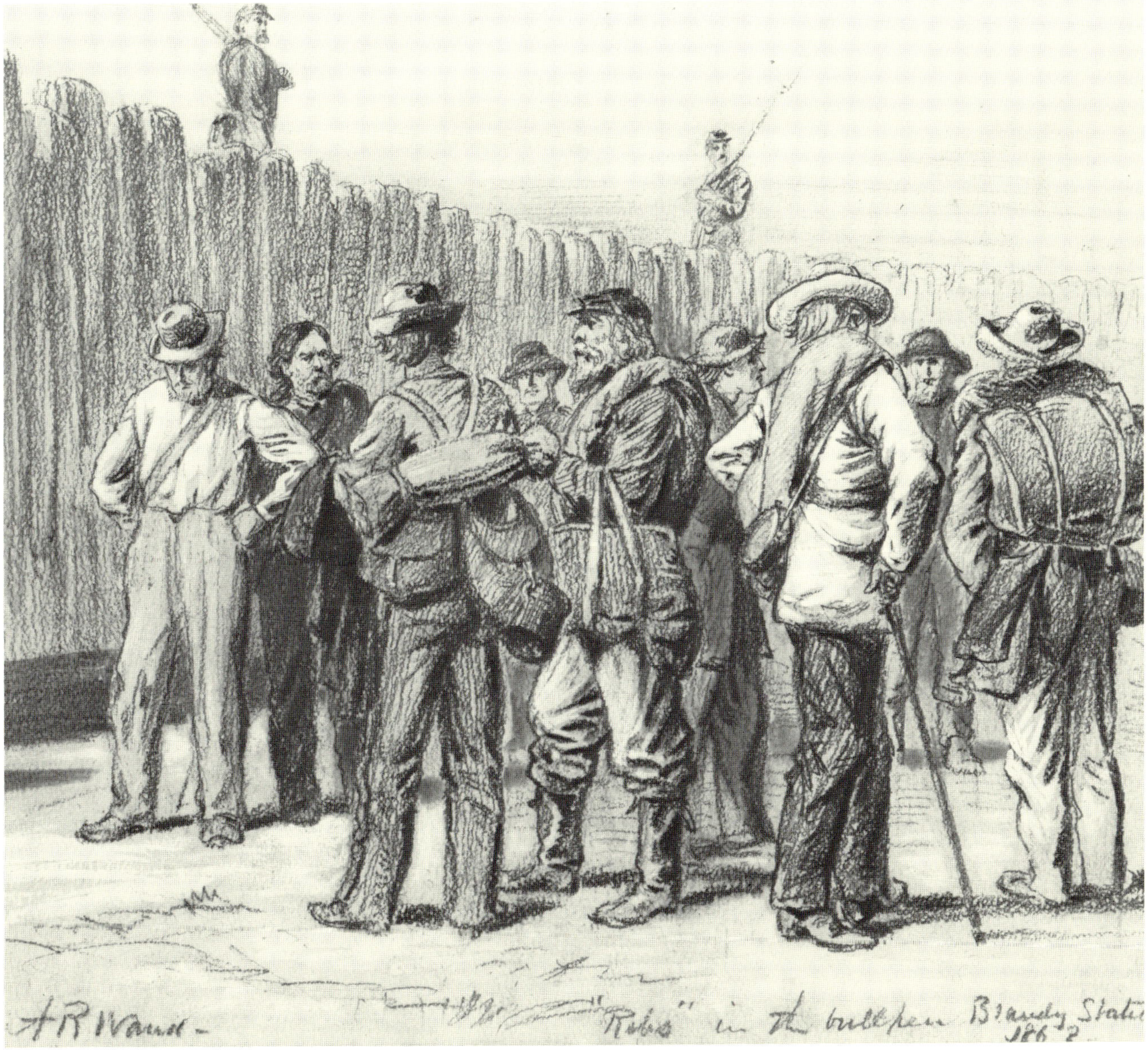
A R Waud -
"Rebs" in the bullpen

No. 41 Robert Walter Weir (1803-1889)

The Letter, 1851
Watercolor; 13 3/4 x 10 7/8 in.

Signed and dated lower left: Robt. W. Weir/ 1851

Weir was born and educated in New York City, apparently a self-taught artist who spent a brief, uninstructed period at the American Academy drawing from the antique, then studied anatomy at New York University's medical school before attempting to paint and market his work. At nineteen one of his pictures was described "as powerful an effort of native talent and true genius as any specimen ever produced in this country by so young an artist." About that time he found a patron in Henry C. Carey, the collector and publisher, who sent him to Italy to further his studies. From 1824 to 1826 he was in Florence and Rome, where he painted several ambitious religious subjects before returning to America with his friend Horatio Greenough. He thereafter exhibited regularly at the National Academy for more than fifty years, from 1827 until 1881, was elected an Associate of the Academy in 1829 and a full Member two years later. A prolific painter, his varied subject matter included portraits, landscapes, as well as history and genre. He became an influential art instructor at West Point's Military Academy in 1834, a post he held until 1876. Whistler was one of his pupils, as well as Generals Grant, Lee, and Sherman. In 1836 he was awarded a national commission to paint *The Embarkation of the Pilgrims* for the Rotunda of the Capitol, undoubtedly the capstone of his career. This typical watercolor shows how Weir combined masterful draftsmanship with skillful handling of a demanding medium to achieve an effective picture.

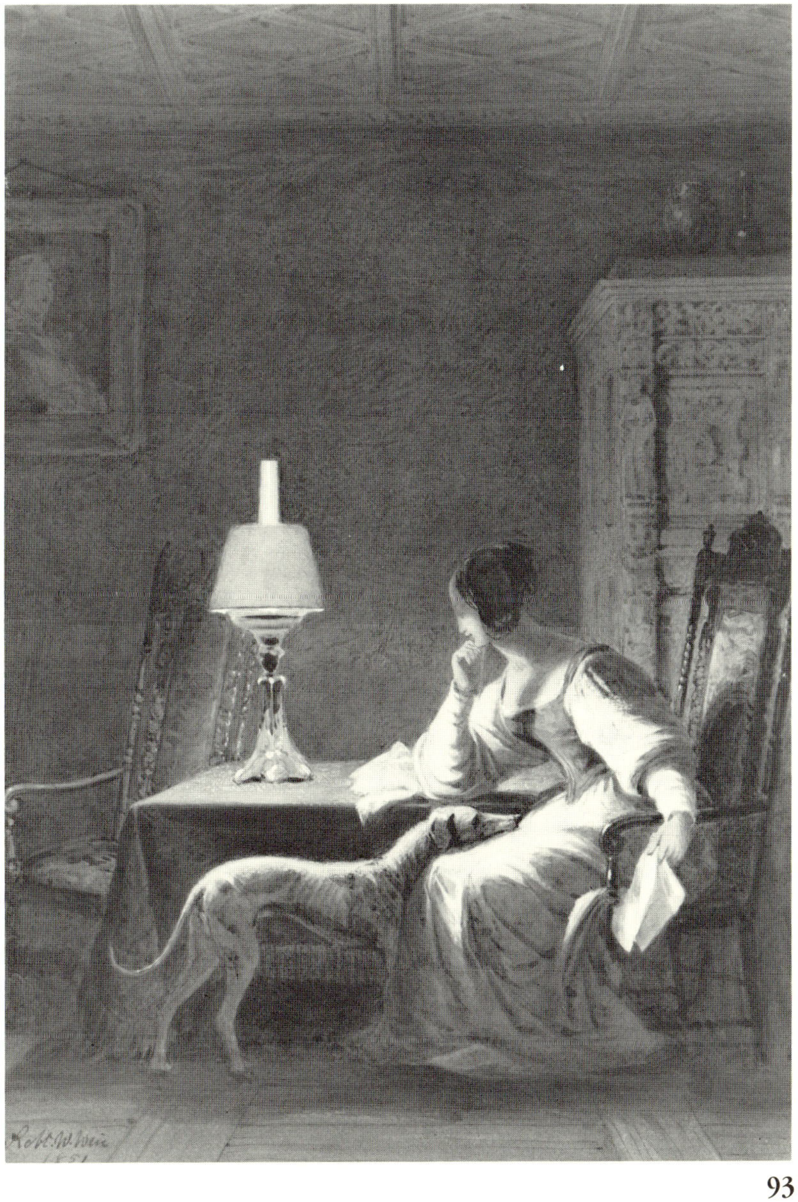

NO. 42 BENJAMIN WEST (1738-1820)

King David Rising After the Death of His Child
Pen and sepia wash on cream paper;
9 5/8 x 14 3/4 in.

Inscribed verso: King David/ Benj[n] West

Lit: H. von Erffa and A. Staley, *The Paintings of Benjamin West* (New Haven and London, Yale University Press, 1986), p. 312.

Prov: Estate of the artist, 1820; auction, Sotheby's, London, June 1, 1839, lot 115 (*Catalogue of 120 Original Drawings by the Late Benjamin West*); Russell B. Mills, Los Angeles, California, 1976-87; Adamson-Duvannes Galleries, Los Angeles, California.

Benjamin West's remarkable career as the first American-born painter to earn a reputation abroad began when he became one of England's most popular painters, a close friend of George III, and a founder of the Royal Academy, all before he reached thirty. In the more than five decades ahead of him, he also became the King's History Painter, succeeded Sir Joshua Reynolds as President of the Royal Academy, and had achieved recognition as one of the most innovative artists of his time. In later years, serious reservations about the quality of his paintings were raised in London art circles, aimed, for the most part, at the prodigious body of work his studio produced for the crown. Although West was received with honor in Paris in 1802, his career at home was already in eclipse. His enduring fame was to rest on his earlier pioneering accomplishment in classical and modern history painting, and on the affection of generations of British and American students who found in his studio a warm reception, encouragement, and generous advice.

With the exception of the finished studies and independent works he occasionally exhibited or gave away, West's drawings were apparently little known and not considered a significant area of his accomplishment. After his death, the drawings remaining in his studio were divided between his two sons. The youngest, Benjamin Jr., organized, identified, and authenticated his personal collection, most probably with some eventual dispersal by auction in mind (a selection of 120 of West's most representative drawings, including this one, was auctioned off at Sotheby's in June, 1839). The holdings of his other son, Raphael,were evidently still mainly intact at the time of his death in 1850, when his wife and daughter presented a number of the drawings to close friends. The bulk of the family collections remained in the hands of descendants on both sides until some twenty-five years ago when they began to appear on the auction market. This was the first time that modern scholarship could begin to re-evaluate West's entire creative work in a new light.

The recognition of West as a prodigy during his formative years in Pennsylvania may have been due in part to his early facility in drawing, but his emergence as a masterly draftsman dates from the time he arrived in London, endowed with an already well established style and working method that quickly impressed everyone. In Italy his disarming manner, humility, and eagerness to learn endeared him to the dilettanti and brought him to the attention of the best resident painters. West's consistent use of drawings to express his ideas and, by stages, to develop his compositions, involved a mature understanding of Renaissance practices he must have learned from artist friends in Rome, particularly Anton Raphael

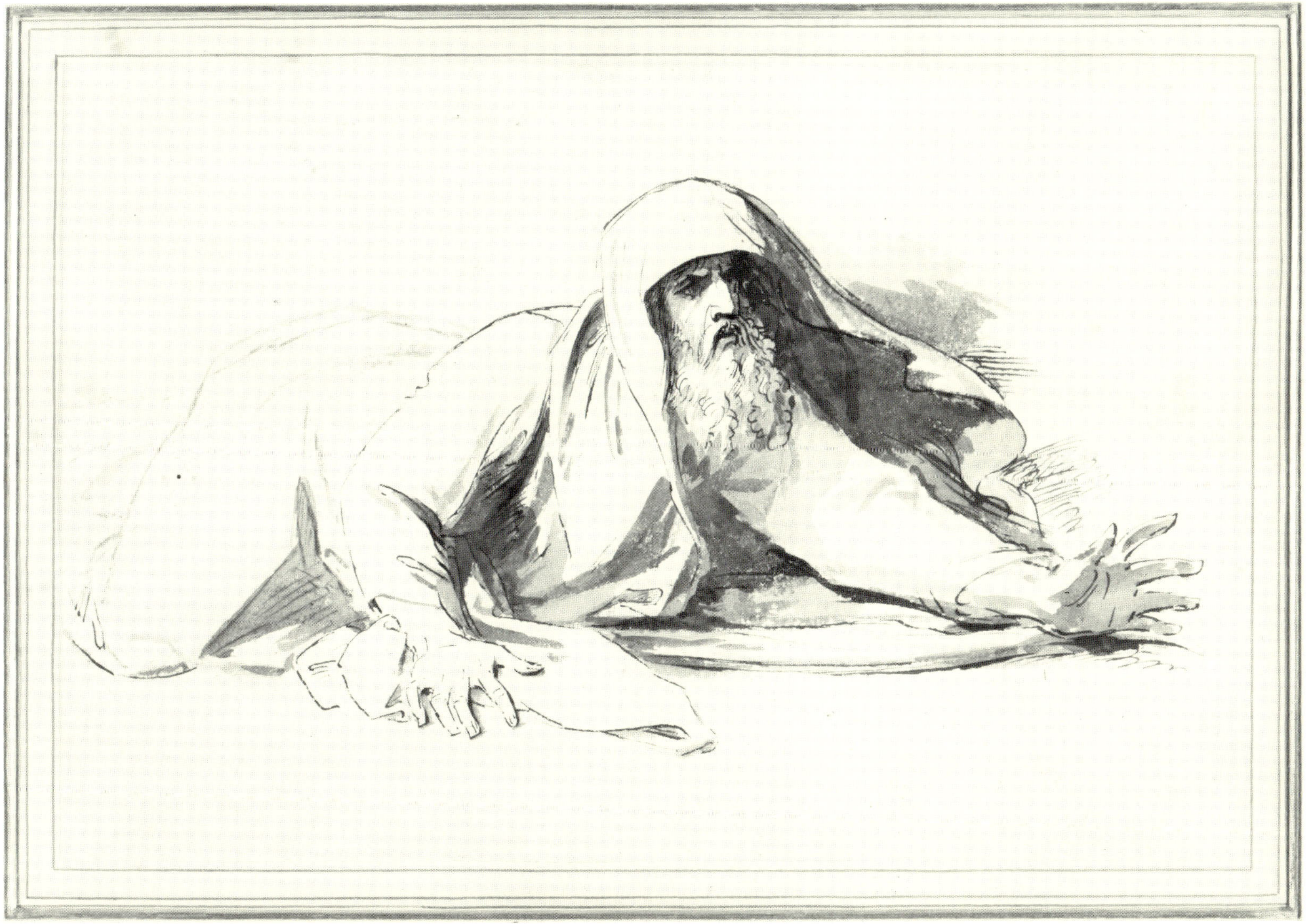

BENJAMIN WEST
(Continued)

Mengs, the great neoclassicist he afterward described as his master. Drawings continued to assume a basic role in his life. Like Reynolds, he also became a celebrated collector of old master drawings. His personal drawing style and technique underwent significant change that also owed much to an intensive study of some of the master draftsmen of the sixteenth and seventeenth centuries represented in his collection. West's own drawings invariably display a variety, freshness, and spontaneity rarely visible in his painting. They present him instead as an entirely new artistic personality. This dramatic drawing relies on a single, monumental figure to illustrate a passage taken from Samuel, Book II, in which a grief-stricken King David is shown slowly rising from the earth after learning of the death of the infant he had fathered adulterously with Bathsheba. The full impact of the moment is told in terms of an abstraction of form, chiaroscuro, expression, and gesture. It was notably one of the drawings Benjamin West, Jr. selected for the auction in 1839.

NO. 43 THOMAS WATERMAN WOOD (1823-1903)

Uncle Ned and I, 1882

Pen and ink on Bristol board;
14 3/8 x 10 3/4 in.

Signed and dated lower left: T. W. Wood/1882

Born in Virginia, Wood's only formal studies in art came when he went to Boston to work under Chester Harding for a year. He afterward followed in Harding's footsteps by working for some ten years as a portrait painter in several east coast cities. The years from 1858 to 1860 he spent abroad, where he studied and copied works of the old masters. On his return he pursued his professional career in the south, chiefly in Tennessee and Kentucky, making portraits and the genre sketches he later developed into paintings. He finally settled in New York where he was to become best known as a painter of sentimental genre and one of the very few artists to concentrate on black subjects with a sympathetic eye. Equally at home in watercolor and graphic media, Wood became president of the Watercolor Society, the National Academy, and one of the founders of the New York Etching Club. He exhibited regularly at the National Academy from 1858 to 1899 and was elected a full Member of the Academy in 1871. This highly finished drawing is closely related to the painting of the same subject Wood exhibited at the Academy in 1882 and was probably produced for publication in Charles M. Kurtz, *National Academy Notes* (New York, Cassell and Co., 1882). The meticulous pen style is also similar to the etching technique Wood used to reproduce several of his paintings. The subject was obviously intended to be autobiographical in nature, in all probability a reminiscence of his Virginia childhood before the Civil War.

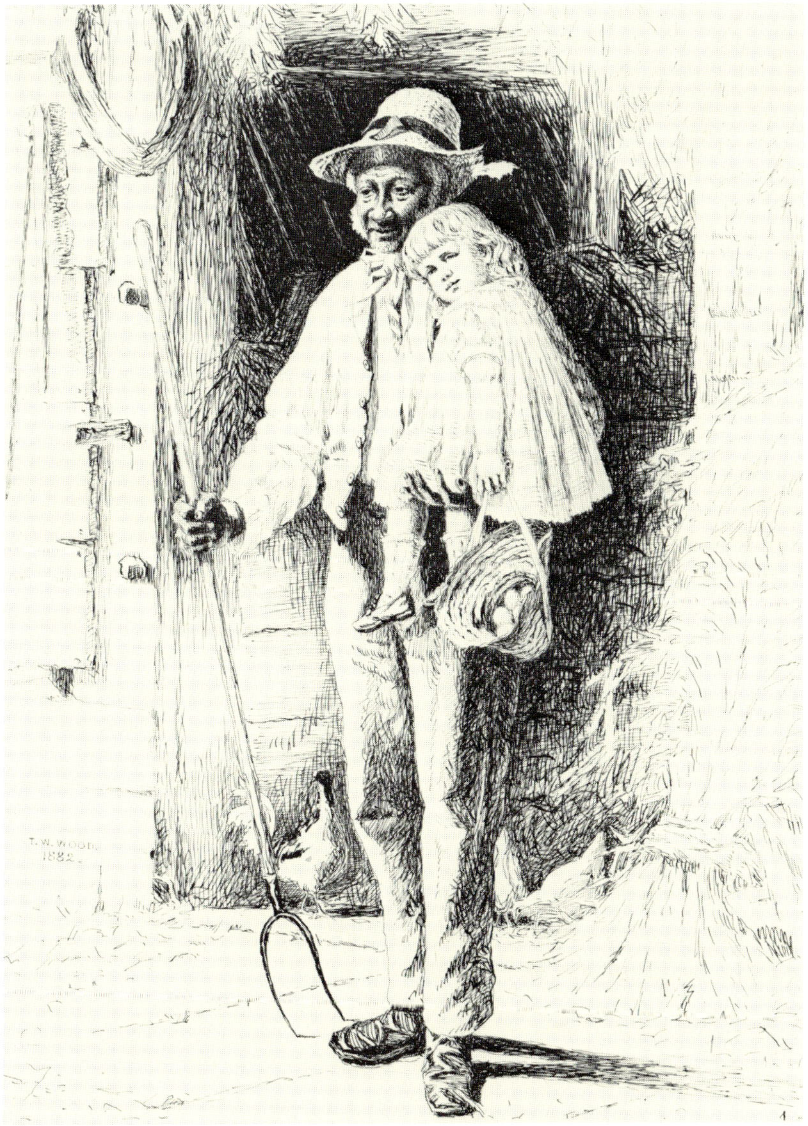
T. W. Wood
1882

Index of Artist	Catalogue Number
Alexander, Esther Frances	1
Brown, Mather	2
Chase, William Merritt	3
Copley, John Singleton	4
Cox, Kenyon	5
Darley, Felix Octavius Carr	6
Davies, Arthur Bowen	7
DuMond, Frank Vincent	8
Falconer, John Mackie	9
Flagg, George Whiting	10
Greenough, Horatio	11
Hawthorne, Charles Webster	12
Henri, Robert	13
Homer, Winslow	14
Hovenden, Thomas	15
Hunt, William Morris	16
Huntington, Daniel	17
Jarvis, John Wesley	18
Johnson, [Jonathan] Eastman	19
La Farge, John	20
Low, Will Hicok	21
Morse, Samuel Finley Breese	22

Index of Artist	Catalogue Number
Mount, William Sidney	23
Myers, Jerome	24
Newell, Hugh	25
Newton, Gilbert Stuart	26
Oertel, Johannes Adam Simon	27
Ranney, William Tylee	28
Rosenthal, Toby Edward	29
Saint-Mémin, Charles Balthazar Julien Fevret de	30
Saintin, Jules Emile	31
Sargent, John Singer	32
Sarony, Napoleon	33
Schussele, Christian	34
Spencer, Lilly Martin	35
Sully, Thomas	36
Thompson, Alfred Wordsworth	37
Vanderlyn, John	38
Vedder, Elihu	39
Waud, Alfred Rudolph	40
Weir, Robert Walter	41
West, Benjamin	42
Wood, Thomas Waterman	43